FROM FEUDALISM TO CAPITALISM

Recent Titles in
Contributions in Political Science

Dependence, Development, and State Repression
George A. Lopez and Michael Stohl, editors

Urban Minority Administrators: Politics, Policy, and Style
Albert K. Karnig and Paula D. McClain, editors

Papers for the Millions: The New Journalism in Britain, 1850s to 1914
Joel H. Wiener, editor

Government Response to Financial Constraints
L. R. Jones and Jerry L. McCaffery

Dilemmas of Social Democracy: The Spanish Socialist Workers Party in the 1980s
Donald Share

A Staff for the President: The Executive Office, 1921–1952
Alfred D. Sander

Hungary and the USSR, 1956–1988: Kadar's Political Leadership
Andrew Felkay

Trotsky and Djilas: Critics of Communist Bureaucracy
Michael M. Lustig

Isolation and Paradox: Defining the "Public" in Modern Political Analysis
Frank Louis Rusciano

The President and Civil Rights Policy: Leadership and Change
Steven A. Shull

Nominating Presidents: An Evaluation of Voters and Primaries
John G. Geer

A Right to Bear Arms: State and Federal Bills of Rights and Constitutional Guarantees
Stephen P. Halbrook

The Politics of Economic Adjustment: Pluralism, Corporatism, and Privatization
Richard E. Foglesong and Joel D. Wolfe, editors

Policy Through Impact Assessment: Institutionalized Analysis as a Policy Strategy
Robert V. Bartlett, editor

Behind the Uprising: Israelis, Jordanians, and Palestinians
Yossi Melman and Dan Raviv

FROM FEUDALISM TO CAPITALISM

Marxian Theories of Class Struggle and Social Change

CLAUDIO J. KATZ

CONTRIBUTIONS IN POLITICAL SCIENCE, NUMBER 239
Bernard K. Johnpoll, *Series Editor*

GREENWOOD PRESS

New York
Westport, Connecticut
London

Library of Congress Cataloging-in-Publication Data

Katz, Claudio J.
From feudalism to capitalism : Marxian theories of class struggle and social change / Claudio J. Katz.
p. cm. — (Contributions in political science, ISSN 0147–1066 : no. 239)
Bibliography: p.
Includes index.
ISBN 0–313–26423–6 (lib. bdg. : alk. paper)
1. Marx, Karl, 1818–1883. 2. Historical materialism. 3. Social conflict. 4. Social change. I. Title. II. Series.
HX39.5.K357 1989
335.4'11—dc20 89–7510

British Library Cataloguing in Publication Data is available.

Library of Congress Catalog Card Number: 89–7510
ISBN: 0–313–26423–6
ISSN: 0147–1066

First published in 1989

Greenwood Press, Inc.
88 Post Road West, Westport, Connecticut 06881

Printed in the United States of America

∞

The paper used in this book complies with the Permanent Paper Standard issued by the National Information Standards Organization (Z39.48–1984).

10 9 8 7 6 5 4 3 2 1

Copyright Acknowledgment

The author and publisher are grateful to International Publishers for granting permission to quote from Karl Marx and Fredrick Engels, *Collected Works*, Moscow: Progress Publishers, 1975–.

In Memory of Dr. Simon Katz

Contents

Acknowledgments

The generous contributions of several individuals have made this study considerably better than it would otherwise have been. Christian Lenhardt commented incisively on several drafts. More importantly, he taught me how to read Marx. Charles A. Miller provided his incomparable critical and editorial gifts. James L. Wiser offered intellectual companionship and patient encouragement throughout. Jill Liske proved to be an invaluable research assistant. Emily Miller made the full resources of the Lake Forest College Library accessible to me. Dean Bailey Donnally offered summer grants which freed me from teaching obligations. I owe an incalculable debt to Sono, whose special understanding for the life of scholarship enabled me to complete this work; and to Daniel, Naomi, and Emma, three children whose lives always help me keep my own in perspective.

1

INTRODUCTION

Speaking to the mourners gathered at Marx's graveside, Engels identified his friend's main achievement as the discovery of the law of development of human history. Comparable in stature, he said, to Darwin's discovery of the law of development of organic nature, Engels summarized Marx's achievement:

> The simple fact . . . that mankind must first of all eat, drink, have shelter and clothing, before it can pursue politics, science, art, religion, etc.; that therefore the production of the immediate material means of subsistence and consequently the degree of economic development attained by a given people or during a given epoch form the foundation upon which the state institutions, the legal conceptions, art, and even the ideas on religion, of the people concerned have been evolved. . . .[1]

This discovery, as Engels points out, underlies Marx's conception of historical change as a response to and consequence of the development of society's productive forces. Marx translated the biological necessity of gaining a livelihood into the historical dominance of technology. The growth of human productive power thus explains the nature and direction of history: social formations rise and fall according as they enable or impede that growth.[2]

This explanation of historical change, however, has an uneasy relationship to another Marxian thesis: that history is the history of class struggle. This view replaces the logic of production with the logic of exploitation at the center of its account of the development of human civilization. The relations of production and the class struggles arising from them, and not the productive forces, determine the internal composition and evolution of social formations in history.

Marx's oscillation between these two principles gave rise to rival versions of historical materialism: one ascribes the fundamental cause of social development to technological progress, the other to class struggle.[3] It should be emphasized that the conflict between them is more profound than whether the direction of the causal chain runs from class to the forces of production or vice versa. These modes of explanation are contradictory: allegiance to one requires essential alterations in the other, specifically, its reformulation in terms of the former's logic. Thus, the technological interpretation of history redefines the notion of class entailed in the thesis that history is class struggle. In turn, the thesis that history is class struggle inverts the relationship between the forces of production and class relations entailed in the technological interpretation. This contradiction, then, cannot be resolved by the familiar appeal to a dialectical interplay between the development of the productive forces and class struggle, for two fundamentally different explanations of historical change are being brought into play. In short, this is a logical and not a dialectical contradiction.[4]

The argument developed in this book is that these two versions of historical materialism are inadequate, both as interpretations of Marx's theory and as explanations of the problems of epochal transitions in history. Marx's writings suggest a conception of radical change that neither version ably captures. Moreover, each version contains theoretical lacunae which impair its usefulness for historical understanding. Marx's own account utilizes forms of explanation which prove more valuable for the analysis of the rise and fall of social formations.

This book offers a reconstruction of Marx's theory of history. "Reconstruction," writes Habermas, "signifies taking a theory apart and putting it back together again in a new form in order to attain more fully the goal it has set for itself. This is the normal way . . . of dealing with a theory that needs revision in many respects but whose potential for stimulation has still not been exhausted."[5] In other words, the reading presented here is discovered in Marx's writings; it was not consciously articulated by Marx. Yet I wish to claim that it is faithful to his intentions. Its constituent categories are taken from Marx's work. But they are interrelated in new ways. The logic of qualitative social transformations developed in these pages is theoretically and historically more tenable than either of the two widely received interpretations of historical materialism.

Our analysis begins with a reconsideration of the respective explanatory roles that the productive forces and class struggle play in Marx's own writings. The argument will move back and forth between a discussion of their rival theoretical claims on the one hand, and the history of the transition from feudalism to capitalism on the other. Underlying this method is the conviction that concepts "will only produce real knowledge if they derive from and return to controllable historical research."[6] The transition to capitalism was chosen to test Marxian theory because it is a principal source from which Marx developed the concepts for interpreting the dynamics of crisis in a mode of production. The reciprocal movement between the two principles of explanation and the historical record seeks to evaluate their relative contributions to an understanding of the supersession of feudalism by capitalism. The result is a new account of the dynamics of crisis and revolutionary transition from one type of society to another.

More specifically, this study distinguishes three different levels of analysis. The first level is that of Marx's self-understanding. Although support for both interpretations of historical materialism can be found in his texts, Marx's own summaries of his theory of history typically award causal primacy to the forces of production. In contrast, it is by now a commonplace of Marx's studies that he nowhere provides an explicit discussion of the concept of class. The second level of analysis is that of Marx's examination of feudalism and the transition to capitalism. Marx's concrete investigations do not always accord with the general framework he developed to account for them. This suggests that Marx did not fully assess his own constructs by testing them against the results of his historical researches, and that his researches were not invariably guided by his theoretical constructs. By contrasting these first two levels, this study seeks to uncover hidden conceptions of historical change that escaped theoretical formulation. The third level of analysis is that of the modern debate on the transition from feudalism to capitalism. Some of the most fruitful controversies in recent historiography address the nature of this transition.[7] Little cross-fertilization takes place between the conceptual clarifications of Marx's work by philosophers and the empirical research of Marxist historians. This study, in contrast, seeks to bridge the debates within these fields. What revisions in Marx's theory of radical social change does the work of modern historians require? And vice versa: do Marx's studies suggest changes in the conclusions these historians have reached?

The claim that Marx's general formulations of historical materialism, which defend a technological interpretation of history, are incompatible with his practice as a historian, where he privileges class struggle, is not uncommon among his interpreters.[8] We shall have occasion to amend this view, however. For while it is true that Marx came to abandon the technological thesis when he actually wrote history, he did so only in his later works, particularly in the *Grundrisse* and *Capital*. This is not to say that Marx's intellectual biography can be read as a linear evolution away from a commitment to the explanatory primacy of the productive forces. For his mature texts continue to adhere to this thesis, albeit only when generalizing about history. These theoretical summations better fit his earlier investigations, however, notably in the *German Ideology*, which explain the development of human civilization, and particularly the transition from feudalism to capitalism, in terms of material progress. Indeed, Marx's most articulate statement of the primacy of the productive forces, he tells us, represents "the general result at which I arrived" in these earlier studies.[9] Marx, then, posited not only distinct principles of historical causation, he wrote distinct histories. There is little point in dwelling on which principle and history Marx preferred; he simply did not integrate the various levels of analysis of his theory of history. Rather, it is more fruitful to assess the heuristic validity of the conflicting versions of his views for historical understanding.

The concluding chapter will venture an explanation of Marx's failure to recognize that he offered incompatible accounts of historical change.

The conception of qualitative social transformation developed in this book will be assessed in terms of its ability to explain the supersession of feudalism by capitalism, a transformation that looms large in Marx's own ideas on radical social change. Its applicability to other epochal changes will not be tested here, however. It is an apposite caution against unwarranted or loose generalizations to note Marx's stricture, given in the course of a comparison between the transition from antiquity to feudalism and from feudalism to capitalism, against erecting "a general historicophilosophical theory, the supreme virtue of which consists in being suprahistorical."[10] Surely, however, the logic of crisis in a mode of production spelled out here will pose questions for the study of other transitions. Needless to add, whether and to what extent the reconstruction of Marx's theory offered below is generalizable awaits further empirical research.

This reconstruction proceeds as follows: Chapter 2 develops and contrasts the two dominant principles of causality in Marx's theory of history: class struggle and the development of the forces of production. Chapter 3 examines the feudal mode of production, assessing the validity of these principles as explanations of its evolution and crisis tendencies. Chapters 4 and 5 explore in detail Marx's interpretation of feudalism's decline and final disintegration, and its replacement by capitalism, providing a critical analysis of the theory of radical social change. Chapter 4 evaluates the thesis of the primacy of the productive forces in precipitating this transition. Chapter 5 examines the applicability of the theory of class struggle in explaining it. The book's conclusion then formulates the new model of qualitative social transformation that emerges from the previous historical studies.

NOTES

1. Engels, "Speech at the Graveside of Karl Marx," in *The Marx-Engels Reader*, ed. Robert C. Tucker, 2d. ed. p. 681.
2. G. A. Cohen, *Karl Marx's Theory of History: A Defence*, p. x.

3. Anderson, *In the Tracks of Historical Materialism*, pp. 33–35. See also Elster, *Making Sense of Marx*, pp. 238–39, 318.

4. Contrast, for example, E. P. Thompson's and G. A. Cohen's interpretations of Marx's now (in)famous statement that "the hand-mill gives you society with the feudal lord; the steam-mill, society with the industrial capitalist." See Marx, *The Poverty of Philosophy*, in Vol. 6 of *Collected Works*, p. 166. (Hereafter *CW*.) Cohen interprets this passage literally, as a blunt statement of the causal primacy of the productive forces. See G. A. Cohen, *Karl Marx's Theory of History*, pp. 41, 96, 144, 163. Thompson, who emphasizes the fundamental role class struggle plays in shaping history, is quite critical of Marx's statement. He argues that the genesis of the factory system in England did not produce, out of whole cloth, a new working class exploited by a capitalist class. Rather, the impact of capitalist industrialization was experienced by ordinary producers with memories of very different modes of work and exploitation. Their past history was critical not only in determining how they received and responded to the introduction of new means of production, but in shaping the process of industrialization itself. See Thompson, *The Making of the English Working Class*, pp. 207–13. In those passages where he underscored the primacy of class, Marx concurs with this assessment. See, for example, Vol. 1 of *Capital*, tr. Moore and Aveling, ed. Engels, p. 402–05.

5. Habermas, *Communication and the Evolution of Society*, tr. McCarthy, p. 95.

6. Anderson, *Arguments Within English Marxism*, p. 66.

7. See in particular the articles now compiled in Hilton, ed., *The Transition From Feudalism to Capitalism*. See also Aston and Philpin, eds., *The Brenner Debate*. This literature is reviewed in chapters 3 through 5 of this study.

8. See, for example, Habermas, *Knowledge and Human Interests*, tr. Shapiro, pp. 25–63 (much the best discussion of this subject). See also Miller, *Analyzing Marx*, pp. 172–73, 205, 217–220.

9. Marx, preface to *A Contribution to the Critique of Political Economy*, in *The Marx-Engels Reader*, p. 4.

10. Marx, Letter to N. K. Mikhailovsky, November 1877, in Marx and Engels, *Selected Correspondence*, 3d. ed. rev., p. 294.

2

The Dynamics of Qualitative Social Transformation

It has often been noted that Marx did not provide an extended treatment of the central concepts of historical materialism. No doubt this is one of the main problems complicating the already difficult task of interpreting Marx's texts: the formal characteristics of his theory of history must be inferred from the various writings in which he addressed this issue in concrete contexts. This book's introduction argued that two incompatible candidates vie for the status of prime mover in Marx's theory—class struggle and technological progress. We now defend this claim. The ideas presented below are developed in two parts. The first addresses Marx's thesis that class formation and struggle explain the historical process; the second examines the thesis investing primacy in the development of the productive forces. These sections reconstruct the central tenets of each thesis, show the sorts of changes the adoption of one requires in the other, and assess their cogency and validity for historical study. The explanatory validity of the concepts elaborated in this chapter are then taken up in the subsequent chapters.

MARX'S THEORY OF CLASS STRUGGLE

Marx's theory that class conflict is the prime mover of historical change is stated in the well-known words of the *Manifesto*:

The history of all hitherto existing society is the history of class struggles.

Freeman and slave, patrician and plebeian, lord and serf, guild-master and journeyman, in a word, oppressor and oppressed, stood in constant opposition to one another, carried on an uninterrupted, now hidden, now open fight, a fight that each time ended, either in a revolutionary re-constitution of society at large, or in the common ruin of the contending classes.[1]

This roll call of classes introduces a complex of issues that has long bedeviled discussions of the Marxian theory of class: (a) The fundamental elements of the concept are obscured by Marx's variable use of the word "class": he uses the term carelessly, often employing it synonymously with faction or group. (b) The connections between the general theory of class, applicable to all class societies, and the concrete analysis of class alignments in particular social formations were never clarified in a theoretically rigorous manner. The first issue to consider here is the nexus between the central, dichotomous class relationship constituting social formations and the plurality of classes which, Marx admits, characterize all historical forms of class society. The second issue is the respective status and position of class and estate as principles of social organization and collective action. The roster of social groups offered in the *Manifesto* mixes together classes with orders and estates, for example, patricians and plebeians. In what sense, then, is class a more basic form of social organization? (c) There is some question whether, for Marx, it is meaningful to think about class as an objective relationship prior to and independent of class consciousness, or whether class consciousness is an essential condition of the existence of class. One of the most controversial aspects of Marx's theory of class is the relationship between class and class consciousness. (d) Marx does not provide a general account of the mechanism whereby class conflict determines the possibilities for economic development and qualitative social change. How does the process of class struggle explain the rise and fall of social formations? The unresolved status of this question in Marx's thought is indicated by the fact that, as Giddens points out, "the struggle between feudal nobility and rising bourgeoisie . . . does not appear in the classification of conflicting classes" opening the *Manifesto*.[2] Yet an understanding of the processes whereby the struggle between lord and serf became the struggle between nobility and bourgeoisie is crucial to an explanation of the revolutionary transition from feudal to capitalist society. These issues will now be taken up in turn.

The Formal Properties of Marx's Concept of Class

Marx's variable use of the term 'class' poses no real difficulty of interpretation. He employed the word in two different senses: a theoretical one and a loose, popular one, obeying both scientific rigor and the verbal conventions of the nineteenth century.[3] For instance, he applies the word to characterize both the proletariat and the intelligentsia, the "ideological classes," described in the *Manifesto* as the "paid wage laborers" of the bourgeoisie, though they are clearly not proletarians in any rigorous sense.[4] What matters is whether this terminological looseness conceals theoretical ambiguities or confusions. Popular usages of the idea of class stress its descriptive connotation: individuals are grouped according to some more or less relevant criterion, for example, income. Positivist social science, emphasizing a nominalist notion of class, has elaborated this aspect of the concept, devising various criteria to rank individuals according to occupational or socioeconomic status. In this view, classes are manifestations of the social structure, derivative of it. When the occasion required it, Marx also used the term this way. The Marxian concept of class has systematic significance, however, only insofar as it identifies groupings of individuals whose interrelationship *constitutes* the social order itself. Class thus provides the key to the internal composition of social formations.

The principal elements of Marx's theory of class are not difficult to distill from his writings. Class is quintessentially a relationship of exploitation and conflict. In each type of class society there are two fundamental classes divided by the antagonistic places they occupy in the network of property rights over persons and productive resources. Specifically, the members of the dominant class enjoy superior terms of access to society's means of production and labor power. They are thereby empowered to determine the conditions of labor of others. The members of the subordinate class are subject to the authority of their superiors, obliged to produce for them. Exploitation thus refers to the extraction of surplus labor from the subordinate producers: they are compelled to transfer an economic surplus beyond what they must produce to satisfy their own needs to the members of the dominant class. In short, the dominant class appropriates a surplus it does not produce; the subordinate class produces a surplus it does not appropriate.

The prevailing relations of effective power over persons and productive resources determine the organizational principle distinguishing modes of production in history. Marx normally uses the concept of a mode of production to identify the combination of a specific set of class relations with a corresponding level of material development—for example, the feudal or capitalist modes of production.

> The specific economic form, in which unpaid surplus-labour is pumped out of direct producers, determines the relationship of rulers and ruled, as it grows directly out of production itself and, in turn, reacts upon it as a determining element. . . . It is always the direct relationship of the owners of the conditions of production to the direct producers—a relation always naturally corresponding to a definite stage in the development of the methods of labour and thereby its social productivity—which reveals the innermost secret, the hidden basis of the entire social structure, and with it the political form of the relation of sovereignty and dependence, in short, the corresponding specific form of the state.[5]

Marx typically distinguishes between three major forms of class subordination—slavery, serfdom, and wage labor.[6] The slaveholder owns and therefore commands the whole of the person of the slave; slaves own neither their own labor power nor the means of production with which they work. Feudal lords enjoy superior but limited rights over the persons and lands of their dependent cultivators. Accordingly, lords are entitled to command only some of the serfs' working days; the remaining days are at the disposal of the direct producers themselves. The capitalist owns none of the person of the wage laborer, but all of the means of production with which he works. Capitalists acquire the right to command labor power because the workers are obliged to exchange it for a livelihood. Accordingly, unlike the serf, the whole of the proletarian's time during which he works is at the disposal of his employer—hence the term "wage slavery."

Class conflict concerns both the right to control the means of production and labor power, and the distribution of socially produced wealth. Clashes over the distribution of wealth are in principle reconcilable in a way clashes over control are not. For if at any given point in time there is only a fixed amount of society's net output to be divided between the contending classes, over an extended period a rising level of output permits them to share out greater amounts. This sort of resolution of class conflict is not uncommon during times of economic growth. Thus, for example, faced with an active peasant resistance, feudal lords were sometimes required to relax the terms of tenure in order to induce cultivators to occupy newly available land. Capitalist growth has often permitted the capitalist class to buy labor peace by granting higher wages. The same result is now achieved in advanced capitalist societies by collective bargaining, whereby employers and workers exchange wage against productivity increases. Economic crises, however, are more apt to open the question of control. This question raises the stakes in the struggle between classes, for control over the means of production and labor power defines the terms of class rule and subordination. Any sort of major extension of class conflict into the area of control therefore poses a threat to the existing class structure.

The theory of class is the focal point of Marx's account of the process of qualitative social transformation. Classes exist in a relationship of "negative reciprocity" in which each is defined and in turn defines itself in opposition to the other. Individuals acquire and maintain the cohesiveness to act and think in class ways only insofar as (or precisely because) they are obliged to defend common interests against a common enemy. Thus, "neither class can escape from the relationship without thereby losing its identity as a distinct class."[7] The success of a subordinate class in elevating itself to a position of dominance comprises a process whereby it necessarily transforms both itself and the social order as a whole. Class struggle thus determines the "law of motion" of historical evolution: its diverse forms and outcomes specify the possibilities for structural change opened by different social formations.

Class and the Analysis of Specific Societies

The class relationships constituting a social formation cannot be given a priori, by definition, but only through empirical analysis of the way surplus labor is appropriated. This is the reason Engels characterized historical materialism as "a guide to study":[8] social constellations have a certain patterned relationship of their own which any mechanistic application of an abstract concept would destroy. Classes in real history do not appear in the highly formalized way in which they are defined by the general model of class relations. Personal dependence under feudalism, for example, assumed a bewildering number of forms which are only imperfectly captured by the term "serfdom." The same is true of the condition of slavery and wage labor. This may explain Marx's hesitation to offer a formal definition of class. Rather, in the role of historian, he employed the abstract concept to interpret concrete social formations. His discussion of the notion of property is instructive:

> In each historical epoch, property has been developed differently and under a set of entirely different social relations. Thus to define bourgeois property is nothing else than to give an exposition of all the social relations of bourgeois production.
>
> To try to give a definition of property as of an independent relation, a category apart, an abstract and eternal idea, can be nothing but an illusion of metaphysics or jurisprudence.[9]

Marx's theory of surplus appropriation informed and guided his historical researches. He acknowledges, however, that only an advanced capitalist system will approximate the "pure" model of a dichotomous class relationship. Capitalist development simplifies class alignments by progressively reducing intervening groups in the population to the conditions of existence of the two polar classes—bourgeoisie and proletariat. Contemporary capitalism, however, presents a complex configuration where "middle and intermediate strata . . . obliterate lines of demarcation everywhere."[10] And earlier epochs manifest "a complicated arrangement of society into various orders, a manifold gradation of rank."[11] Accordingly, whereas the relationship of surplus extraction constitutes the organizing principle of all modes of production, the main class system is complicated by secondary groupings in all historical forms of class society.

What, then, is the nature of the connections between the general model of class, applicable to all types of class society, and the concrete study of class relationships in specific contexts? Marx recognizes three main types of "complicating" groupings: (a) Transitional classes, either rising classes under the waning rule of the dominant class relationship, for example, the nascent bourgeoisie in late medieval Europe, or declining classes destined to dissolve within a new social formation, but which still retain certain vestiges of their traditional power, for example, the aristocracy in capitalist Europe.[12] (b) Marginal classes inhabiting the fringes of the central class relationship: these social groups do not represent past or anticipate future class systems; rather, they are sectors indigenous to but increasingly marginalized by the evolution of their societies. Marx designates the petty bourgeoisie as an increasingly peripheral class in capitalist society.[13] (c) Lastly, Marx is well aware that classes are not homogeneous formations but relationships composed of "various fractions," that is, sectors and subdivisions, whose interests are often at odds with one another.[14]

Transitional classes are clearly of primary significance here, for they constitute the dialectic of rising and declining classes attending epochal historical transformations. This particular constellation is the result of the collision between rival modes of production within a single social formation, for example, the ancien regime.[15] Marx's study of the rise of the bourgeoisie from its genesis in late feudal Europe to mature capitalist class reflects a recognition that radical historical change does not occur all at once but "only very slowly; the various stages and interests are never completely overcome, but only subordinated to the prevailing interest and trail along beside the latter for centuries afterwards."[16] Alfred Cobban is therefore mistaken when he suggests that, for Marx, a rising class is one which "acquires political power and increased economic well-being and yet remains the same class."[17] Rather, classes in transition evolve as a succession of fractions which gain precedence within them in a process of formation. Accordingly, Marx identifies rising and declining groups *within* transitional classes. The changing configuration of sectors specifies their internal composition at different points in their history, reflecting both the trajectory of their struggle and the nature of the social transformation it precipitates: "The class rises as the various forms in which its centre of gravity has lain at different times are ruined and with them the different sections whose influence derives from these forms. In my view, this sequence of metamorphoses [leads] up to the domination of the class. . . . "[18]

The history of the bourgeoisie reveals yet a fourth factor complicating the pure model of class, namely, its relationship to estates. Marx argues that, like other types of class society, feudal society represented "an association against a subjected producing class."[19] Yet he often equates feudal society with estate society, maintaining that "the emergence of . . . class . . . is . . . a product of the bourgeoisie."[20] The question raised here concerns the significance of the formation of markets for the study of class relations. Does class identify the organizational principle of pre-capitalist societies, or is class less essential to understand them? Are precapitalist societies best understood by supplementing or even replacing class analysis with another principle of social organization recognizing social groupings such as order or estate?

The uncertainty surrounding the relationship between estate and estate society, and class and class society, revolves in part around the ambiguity inherent in the notion of the "economy." Its modern definition is a legacy of the bourgeoisie: it refers to the nexus of activities of market participants. *Homo economicus* is a rational utilitarian motivated not by the gain of power, but by the power of gain. Clearly, the assumption that class is an economic category in this sense makes nonsense of any attempt to apply it to precapitalist societies.[21] But Marx took leave of the narrow economism of classical political economy for a definition of the economic structure as a society's relations of power over persons and productive resources.

Only in a capitalist society does economy in the broad sense assume the form of an economy in the narrow sense. The bourgeois property order has shed its political skin: surplus is extracted by means of the free labor contract. Wage laborers have the unique attribute of being the sole proprietors of their capacity to work while being denied ownership of the means of production with which they work. In contrast, slaves own neither their labor power nor their means of production; peasants have some rights in both, although they are compelled to transfer given amounts of their labor and its product to the lord. Thus, the precapitalist "property relationship [necessarily] . . . appears as a direct relation of lordship and servitude, so that the direct producer is not free." Surplus is appropriated "by other than economic pressure," that is, through juridical-political means supported by tradition and sanctioned in the final analysis by manifest force.[22] *This* is the system which denotes the class structure of precapitalist societies. For example, the complex of private jurisdictions defining the privileges of the medieval nobility had a concrete practical meaning: it comprised the greater part of the levers whereby the members of the feudal ruling class extracted an economic surplus from the direct producers. The peasantry thus showed sound class sense when it sought to dismantle these privileges.[23]

Class rather than estate or order is therefore a more basic principle of social organization because it specifies the social incidence of effective rights to command labor power and its product, and thus apportions the chances for the satisfaction of socially privileged needs:

> Where men are divided into classes by their mode of sustaining life, it is through class and in reference to it that they generally seek "rank", "standing", "status", and "security"; at the very least, the obstacles to the achievement of these goals and the means of achieving them will vary according to class.[24]

Class is thus not the sole category of social stratification; nevertheless, it remains true that "the existence of other social classifications does not . . . render the category of class less essential," for "these other categories cannot themselves be understood except in light of class."[25]

Class Consciousness

Among Marx's less systematic statements on class, two have attracted considerable attention.[26] The controversy turns on whether Marx distinguished "a class in itself" from "a class for itself," sharply differentiating an objective definition of class from its subjective expressions in struggle and consciousness. G. A. Cohen has provided a forceful defense of the structural conception: "A person's class is established by nothing but his objective place in the network of ownership relations. . . . His consciousness, culture, and politics do not enter the *definition* of his class position." A note adds: "Not even his behaviour is an essential part of it."[27] A strict distinction between structure and consciousness is required, first, "to protect the substantive character of the Marxian thesis that class position strongly conditions consciousness, culture, and politics."[28] Second, the distinction is needed to rescue the universal applicability of class analysis for historical study. If class consciousness is the touchstone of class, it is argued, the concept ceases to have any heuristic validity for periods when no class consciousness can be discerned. "It is precisely because a class need *not* be conscious of itself," writes Cohen, "that the phrase 'class-in-itself' was introduced."[29]

E. P. Thompson, in contrast, develops the thesis that class is the historical outcome of complex processes of formation in which struggle and consciousness play a determining role. He argues that the structural definition impoverishes historical understanding, and adds that Marx did not countenance its usage, although he declines to establish this last claim.[30] We now argue that Thompson is in fact correct: Marx's notion of class is the one he—not Cohen—recommends.

For Marx, the importance of class is grounded on the premise that the concept has explanatory and not merely descriptive validity for historical analysis. In contrast to positivist social science, which typically treats class as a purely theoretical construct, a creation of the observer, Marx is concerned to make class visible in history as a real phenomenon. For Marx, that is, the concept of class is meaningful only insofar as it permits an interpretation of social formations *in terms* of class struggle. The structural definition of class, however, undermines its explanatory validity. Anderson, for example, summarizes the structural conception thus: "It is, and must be, the dominant mode of production that confers fundamental unity on a social formation, allocating their objective positions to the classes within it, and distributing the agents within each class. *The result is, typically, an objective process of class struggle* [emphasis added]."[31] Anderson makes a precipitous leap from individuals' economic position to their class behavior: "The result is . . . an objective process of class struggle." There are two dangers in this conception. First, it suggests that classes are present in social formations by definition. There appears to be little need for a study demonstrating how individuals in determinate production relations come to engage in collective struggles which shape social reality. Without this study, however, class is reduced to a purely nominal category, imposed upon the evidence.[32] Nothing Marx writes, to be sure, suggests that class is only a cultural phenomenon, independent of its structural moorings. But the identification of objective class locations, however precisely and completely, is only the beginning of historical study. What must then be addressed is the question of class formation, the processes whereby individuals acquire a capacity for collective action. This is the question which raises the most important and problematic issues about class. Indeed, only its answer can vindicate the explanatory power of the concept, by reconstructing the ways in which class struggles impose their pattern on history.[33]

Secondly, the structural definition of class suggests that a class's behavior and consciousness can be deduced from its objective place in the economy by means of a simple equation. To be sure, Cohen accepts the argument, and surely Anderson agrees, that "the connection between production relations on the one hand and consciousness, politics, and culture on the other is not simple. There is logic in it but not law."[34] The austerity of the structural premise—that a person's class is established by nothing but his objective place in the network of ownership relations—is nevertheless belied by the study of class formation. For this study shows that consciousness, politics and culture constitute the terms in which individuals interpret and respond to their economic situation. These elements can therefore not be understood, however undogmatically, as subjective expressions of their situation, but enter into their coming together as a class. In an important sense, Marx inverts the structural conception, suggesting that class struggle *precedes* class. For men and women discover their shared predicament and articulate a common language and action, thus coming into existence as a class, only in the process of defending their interests against other men and women who occupy an antagonistic position in the relations of production. Outside the boundaries of this struggle, the combatants tend to lose their cohesion as classes.[35]

Is this interpretation of class invalidated by historical evidence of individuals bound by similar production relations who nevertheless fail to identify their interests as a class? Marx's structural interpreters suggest that he developed the notion of class in itself to retain the usefulness of class analysis in these cases, for example, a study of the peasantry. The problem, however, is not so much in the historical evidence as in the poverty of the categories used to understand it. The distinction between class in itself and for itself needlessly restricts the range of possible degrees and types of class formation and consciousness: it implies that individuals are either fully aware of their class as a historical actor, or they do not struggle and think in class ways, even if they remain—structurally—a class.[36] It is the structural definition, then, which robs the concept of its heuristic validity for historical study.

For Marx, on the contrary, classes are historical relationships involving complex processes of formation and disintegration. Indeed, he nowhere uses the term class in itself, or contrasts it with a class for itself.[37] Scholars attributing this distinction to Marx have misread the two passages adduced to support it. In the first, from *The Poverty of Philosophy*, Marx distinguishes between the proletariat insofar as it constitutes "a class as against capital," and a class "for itself."[38] This distinction denotes two levels of working class struggle: it refers, first, to the workers' attempts to resist capitalist exploitation, specifically to maintain wages, and second, to their endeavor to construct a wholly new society. Marx simply does not refer to the proletariat as a class in itself, independently of struggle and consciousness.

In the second passage, from *The Eighteenth Brumaire of Louis Bonaparte*, Marx draws a distinction between peasants insofar as "they do not form a class," and insofar as they do "form a class."[39] The context of this passage shows that Marx is not referring solely to the nineteenth century French peasantry. Rather, he draws a distinction between the conditions of peasant existence prior to and following the French Revolution and Napoleonic Wars. The prerevolutionary peasantry formed a cohesive bloc demonstrating a talent for organization and united action well-known to historians. Marx assigns peasant class struggle an essential role in dismantling the ancien regime.[40] Following the Revolution, however, the peasantry rapidly lost its capacity for concerted, sustained struggle, precisely because the seigneur, the traditional antagonist against whom its solidarity had been forged, was defeated.[41] By the mid-nineteenth century, Marx argues, it could no longer enforce its "class interests in [its] own name;" it was clearly "incapable of any revolutionary initiative."[42] But Marx's carefully couched language indicates that he is far from the view that the peasantry disintegrated into a class in itself, losing all residual capacity to struggle or think in class ways. This conception would indeed deny him the possibility of explaining the peasantry's intervention in mid-century French society and politics: an inert structure disallows an account of the history of concrete struggles.

Marx contends that the peasant class was mainly responsible for Louis Bonaparte's rise to power. He vindicates this thesis by investigating how the peasantry came to acquire real historical existence as one of the principal agents shaping the social formation. His study makes it clear that capitalism's transformation of French agriculture cannot be conceived as a blind process reallocating the peasants within new relations of production, assigning blank and passive human beings their objective class positions. Nor can the peasants' support for Napoleon be deduced from their situation. Napoleon's rise to power confronted Marx with a profound puzzle, which the peasantry's class position could not easily resolve. Rather, Marx explains the peasants' collective behavior in terms of their shared experience and the historical and cultural characteristics which shaped it. He shows that capitalist exploitation confronted individuals with living memories of their own. These historical traditions provided the terms in which the peasants made sense of their objective circumstances and articulated their common interests. Specifically, Marx argues that French peasants interpreted their present situation against the background of their revolutionary experience of 1789. The Napoleonic Code had given them ownership rights to their plots, precisely those rights which capitalist exploitation threatened. When the crisis of the mid-nineteenth century again propelled the peasants onto the French political stage, they responded by recalling the name they associated with their golden age.[43]

The distinction between class in itself and class for itself fails to explain peasant class behavior either before or after the Revolution. In both situations the peasantry came to struggle and define itself in (albeit different) class ways, and yet in neither situation did it develop a consciousness of itself as a distinct class. It is more useful, then, to distinguish between class consciousness—expressions of class identity, which can take many forms, for instance, class specific interpretations of dominant ideologies[44]—and consciousness of class, that is, a class's awareness of its precise place and role in the historical process.[45] Class consciousness is an integral part of the definition of class. For Marx, however, consciousness of class is first made possible by capitalist society, and only the proletariat is fully capable of becoming a class for itself. It is in this sense that he argues that the emergence of class is a product of the bourgeoisie.[46]

It is sometimes argued that Marx demonstrated his commitment to the structural reading of class by restricting the role of class struggle and consciousness to the surface relief of society. In this view, the analysis of a specific historical conjuncture does indeed require a focus on class struggle and the superstructural expressions of class. Hence Marx examines conflicts, shifting alliances, the organization and disorganization of classes primarily in his historical case studies, because these struggles provide the immediate explanation of contemporary events—for instance, Louis Napoleon's rise to power. But an explanation of the underlying structure and development of society requires a study of more fundamental economic processes below the direct confrontation between classes.[47]

This interpretation is unwarranted. Marx clearly adheres to the thesis that economic relations, in the form of a mode of exploitation, constitute the ground of class struggle. But he also shows that the long-term course of class conflict structures economic relations and determines the nature of major social transformations. We shall argue that the outcomes of feudal class struggles played a large role in conditioning the distinct paths from feudalism to capitalism taken by England and France and the specific historical form and trajectory of the new mode of production in each country. In sum, the history of class struggles explains both the surface relief of society and its long-term processes of development, crisis, and transition to a new form of society.

Class Struggle and Economic Development

The central question of Marx's materialist view of history is: What is the primary motor of economic change? The technological interpretation of Marx's answer maintains that the level of development of the productive forces explains the viability of social formations in history. On this view, history is the story of how class relations adapt to the requirements of material progress, facilitating technological improvements. In contrast, the thesis that history is the story of class struggle states that the nature of class relations constituting a social formation explains its level and rate of productive development. This thesis has not been systematically developed.

Reconstructions of Marx's theory of class have typically focused on how classes make themselves in history. Less attention has been paid to how history is made by classes. Indeed, Jon Elster has written that Marx offers "no hint of any mechanism by which the class struggle promotes the growth of the productive forces."[48] We now argue against this proposition. To be sure, Marx did not provide a general discussion of this issue.

But his understanding of the mechanisms whereby class antagonism governs material progress can nevertheless be distilled from his mature historical writings, particularly in the *Grundrisse* and *Capital*.

A class's impact on economic development is rooted in the logic of class struggle. Class conflict arises from the system of exploitation, in which control of the means of production entails the right to allocate labor power and its product. Individuals come to organize and struggle as classes principally to protect and defend common conditions of existence. This is the chief reason they develop and maintain various types of class based institutions—for example, peasant village organizations, labor unions—whose purpose is to impose a certain discipline on their members and coordinate their activities: these are indispensable prerequisites of successful struggle.

How, then, do the contending classes pursue their interests? What is the most rational way of doing so? Their strategies depend on the prevailing mechanisms of surplus extraction. The dominant class's predominant interest lies in reproducing these mechanisms. Specifically, its members are obliged to protect their capacity to appropriate a surplus, both from rivals within their own class and from the subordinate class. They are thus compelled to use the lion's share of the surplus they extract to preserve and improve the means to extract additional surplus. Economic growth is a function of the size and use of socially produced wealth. Increases in productivity are achieved when surplus product is applied to expanding and improving society's productive forces. Ruling classes, then, promote economic progress only when and to the extent that using surplus to reproduce the existing instruments of exploitation coincides with using it to reproduce the instruments of production.

The form and intensity of the direct producers' resistance to the demands made on them is the other major factor determining how socially produced wealth is distributed and to what ends it is applied. Individuals within the subordinate class employ the surplus they succeed in retaining to reproduce their material conditions of life. How they use this surplus depends on their position as a class. Do they have direct access to the means of production? They will then be in a position to improve their material well-being by improving the productive forces. Hence Marx argues that the medieval peasantry provided the main impetus for feudal economic growth.[49] Proletarians, in contrast, do not have direct access to the means of production. The major portion of the surplus they succeed in retaining is directed to consumption. Effective demand, however, only makes an indirect contribution to capitalist development.

The way in which people use their economic resources to improve their material circumstances does not necessarily correspond to the use of these resources to maximize productivity. Each is governed by qualitatively different principles. The economic activities in which individuals must participate to improve their circumstances are determined by their class position, that is, by the nature of their rights over labor power and tangible wealth. But the economic activities in which they would have to participate to maximize the rate of economic growth entail the development and implementation of new productive techniques. Whether and with what degree of efficiency a society searches for and applies new techniques depends upon the strategies the members of its constituent classes are required to adopt in their endeavor to maintain historically conditioned modes of life. Rational economic behavior is defined by their needs and capacities as members of a class, not by the "needs" or "powers" of the forces of production. Thus, capitalism's prodigious productivity is sustained by the imperatives of its appropriation process, which channel the vast proportion of the surplus it generates into the development of physical plant and equipment. Capitalists are obliged to invest to preserve the conditions of continued surplus extraction; the market ensures that those who fail to compete go under. By contrast, the feudal aristocracy depended upon extraeconomic means of coercion to siphon a surplus from the peasantry.[50] Feudal lords thus used their wealth to maintain the military and political complex that buttressed their class power. They allocated the surplus they extracted to sustain policies of war and magnificence, neither of which made sustained contributions to productive development. The nature of feudal class rule therefore constrained growth within narrow bounds.[51]

A crisis in a mode of production occurs when the economic

strategies individuals adopt to improve their material conditions collide with the reproduction of the productive forces. A social contradiction, Marx argues, comprises a situation in which the uses of surplus product individuals must make to defend their class position undermine the development of the forces of production; or, inversely, when the necessary investments of surplus they must make to maintain the productive forces impair their class power. Contradictory imperatives in the process of surplus appropriation eventually undermine the preconditions of the process itself. Thus, for example, the most rational way for capitalists to appropriate surplus value is to introduce labor-saving techology. Yet this strategy is at once necessary to defend their capacity to extract a surplus and self-destructive, for the replacement of living labor by machinery narrows the base from which additional surplus can be drawn.[52] Similarly, the preservation of feudal class power required lords to improve the extraeconomic complex of military and political coercion. Accordingly, the lords siphoned more surplus from the peasant economy than they returned to it in the form of productive investments, eventually crippling its ability to produce any surplus.[53] With the erosion of the preconditions of surplus appropriation, the motive force of economic development falters and stalls. The resulting crisis manifests itself in a contraction of society's material base.

The general depression is surmounted only when class relations are restored or revamped. A particularly severe crisis may result in a restoration of the dominant class system, but in an altered form. Thus, for example, following the fourteenth century crash, feudal economic growth resumed again in the sixteenth century, but only once feudal class relations were stabilized by the nascent absolutist monarchies.[54] Similarly, the great capitalist world crash of the early twentieth century put an end to capitalism's liberal phase; the economic miracle following World War II occurred under the auspices of a state regulated capitalist economy. Or, in the event that the crisis results in the qualitative transformation of the dominant class system, economic growth resumes under the imperatives of the new class system: for example, the transition from feudal to capitalist class relations witnessed in the English countryside in the sixteenth and seventeenth centuries enabled the increases in agricultural productivity that eventually underwrote England's industrial revolution.

This explanation of the nature of social crises is incompatible with Marx's more familiar account, given in the technological interpretation of historical materialism. The widely received view is that crises are the result of a collision between growing productive forces and increasingly obsolete class relations, wherein the tension between them is resolved in favor of the forces, by a qualitative change in the relations. A defense of the thesis that history is class struggle turns this conception upside down: Crises are the result of contradictions inherent in the dominant class system which disrupt the reproduction of the productive forces, crippling material life. These contradictions may in fact culminate in a prolonged regression of society's productive power—for example, the severe economic deterioration which attended both the decline of the Roman Empire and the crisis which convulsed feudal Europe in the fourteenth century. Only *prior* changes in class relations permit the emergence of new productive forces.[55] The nascent class system determines the possibilities for productive development: there is no suggestion in this view that the new ruling class will necessarily encourage optimal growth, and no hint that it emerged in order to do so.[56]

Under what conditions, then, is a class created with the capacity and the interest to transform society as a whole? Marx's theory of class struggle does not answer this question in a sufficiently rigorous fashion. One of the ways to identify its ambiguities is to return to the catalogue of class conflicts with which Marx opens the first part of the *Manifesto*: "Freeman and slave, patrician and plebeian, lord and serf, guild-master and journeyman, in a word, oppressor and oppressed, stood in constant opposition to one another. . . . " These struggles culminate "either in a revolutionary re-constitution of society at large, or in the common ruin of the contending classes."[57] The theory of class is thus tied to the transformation of types of society: A successful revolutionary class destroys the system of exploitation oppressing it, constituting itself as an alternative ruling class.[58]

It has been pointed out, however, that this catalogue of class conflicts omits the struggle between aristocracy and bourgeoisie, precisely the struggle that propelled the transition from feudalism to capitalism. The reason, we shall argue, is that a fundamental difference exists between the class systems characterized as "oppressor and oppressed" and the conflict between the feudal and nascent capitalist classes. The omission, in other words, suggests a distinction between two types of class struggle. On the one hand, the antagonism characterizing Marx's catalogue of class conflicts, for example, lord and serf, arises out of the nexus of exploitation between an appropriating and a producing class. On the other hand, the antagonism between aristocracy and bourgeoisie represents a class conflict between irreconcilable owners of the means of production, that is, between two appropriating classes struggling to secure the dominance of differing modes of surplus extraction. The main difference between these two types of class conflict may be schematically stated thus: The former involves the struggle *within* a mode of production, arising out of the conflict of interest within a single class-based system; the contending classes clash over the *distribution* of surplus produced in a given economy. The latter involves the antagonism *between* modes of production, deriving from a clash between class systems; class conflict here concerns the *mode* whereby surplus is produced. These two types of class conflict are qualitatively different: they have distinct sources and they are governed by different dynamics. More importantly, they resolve themselves in different ways. Class conflict within a mode of production typically ends not in "a revolutionary re-constitution of society at large," but rather "in the common ruin to the contending classes."[59] By contrast, the clash between class systems culminates in the formation of a wholly new society and economy. One of the most important issues facing a class analysis of radical historical change, then, is to account for the processes whereby the conflict within a mode of production transforms itself into the conflict between modes of production.

The usefulness of this distinction will be tested in an examination of the collapse of West European feudalism and its supersession by capitalism. This study shows that the theory of class struggle must be substantially refined to rescue its explanatory validity. Yet these refinements are implicit in Marx's own historical researches, that is, in what he actually wrote concerning the transition from feudal to capitalist society.

THE TECHNOLOGICAL INTERPRETATION OF HISTORICAL MATERIALISM

Marx's conception that history is the story of humanity's progressive conquest of nature is, unlike that assigning primacy to class struggles, explicitly stated in his writings. The view that Marx intended to ascribe centrality to technological development, however, has attracted considerable controversy. One common criticism is that this reading rests on occasional and allusive passages in Marx's texts, notably on the preface to *A Contribution to the Critique of Political Economy*, in which he offered compressed digests of his theory of history. A related criticism is that, as a practicing historian, Marx freely abandoned this approach.[60] Neither objection is warranted. To be sure, Marx's statements of the primacy of the forces of production are typically offered as summaries of concrete historical analyses, but they are neither so rare nor so allusive as critics claim. Indeed, G. A. Cohen has compiled extensive textual evidence of Marx's commitment to this thesis, and provided a cogent reconstruction of its central tenets.[61] Moreover, only Marx's mature economic histories show little allegiance to the primacy of the productive forces; his earlier historical investigations, in contrast, offer an extended defense of the fundamental, independent role that material progress plays in explaining historical change.

The technological interpretation of historical materialism states that the level of development attained by the productive forces explains the central features of a society's relations of production. Its defense requires answers to four questions: (a) Does Marx offer a criterion permitting a clear demarcation of the forces of production from the relations of production? A prevalent objection to the technological interpretation states that Marx and his followers include relations of production among the productive forces and yet claim to explain the relations by appealing to the forces. (b) Marx makes repeated references to the profound influence of the relations on the forces of production. What, then, is the nature of the primacy of the productive forces? (c) Where does class struggle fit in? The technological reading is often accused of removing the subject from history, ascribing needs and agency to the forces of production. (d) What is the definition of class required by the thesis that history is material progress? Marx's interpreters have often noted the disjuncture in his writings between two versions of historical materialism. What is rarely noted is that Marx employs two conceptions of class: one corresponds to the primacy of the productive forces, the other to the primacy of class struggle.

Forces and Relations of Production

Marx uses the following criterion to distinguish the forces of production from the relations of production: The forces of production enable human beings to exploit nature, the relations enable them to exploit other human beings. The forces of production encompass the means people use to transform and control nature, adapting it to satisfy their needs.[62] As such, they consist of the available means of production, including the existing technology (tools and machinery), physical facilities and raw materials, but the primary force here is the scientific knowledge that yields productive power. Secondly, the productive forces comprise the qualifications of the labor power available for setting the means of production to work, here mainly the physical and technical capabilities of the workforce.[63]

The relations of production specify the distribution of power in society. For Marx, social power is ultimately grounded in enforceable claims over persons and material resources. Superior claims enable individuals to command the distribution of labor power and its product. The relations of production thus give rise to the nexus of exploitation comprising social classes. They need not be class relations, however: neither very primitive communal societies nor the anticipated socialist societies are characterized by class divisions.[64] They assume the form of class relations when the property system empowers a set of individuals to determine the terms of access to society's means of production, permitting them to control the conditions of labor of others.

There is considerable controversy regarding where Marx located the division of labor within a society's overall structure.[65] This uncertainty is due in part to the fact that the concept has a dual meaning in Marx's writings. On the one hand, it refers to the authority structure required to direct a given unit of production—that is, to the relationship between those who give and those who receive commands, including the prevailing means of enforcing labor discipline. In this sense, the division of labor belongs within the relations of production. Marx characterized the division between mental and manual labor as a class division.[66] On the other hand, it refers to the specialization and coordination of tasks within units of production, defined apart from the control over people and material resources, and to the separation between units of production within society as a whole. In this sense, the division of labor must be included within the productive forces.

Marx characterized the relations between individuals engaged in production thus:

> Social [production] . . . denotes the co-operation of several individuals, no matter under what conditions, in what manner and to what end. It follows from this that a certain mode of production, or industrial stage, is always combined with a certain mode of co-operation, . . . and this mode of co-operation is itself a "productive force."[67]

In Marx's view, the mode of cooperation develops in conjunction with the divisison of labor within society at large. Both play a direct role in humanity's progressive mastery of nature. Greater specialization and coordination of tasks among individuals who work together not only increases the productive power of each individual laborer, but creates a wholly new power, the combined power of the collective laborer.[68] The differentiation of new spheres of production permits each sphere to develop according to its own comparative economic advantage. Hence the extension of commerce is historically significant because it promotes the process of differentiation among industries and among economic regions, beginning with the separation of town and country and culminating in a world division of labor.[69] Accordingly, Marx argued that some of the most important improvements in society's productive forces took the form of improvements in the division of labor, the actual means of production remaining virtually unaltered. He assigned these changes in the organization of the work process an independent role in explaining the advent of new class relations. The shift from petty handicraft industry to manufacture, for example, represented an epochal economic advance, furthering the rise of capitalist class relations.[70] This development, however, entailed essentially a revolution in the allocation of tasks, not in existing productive techniques, which played a decidedly subordinate role.[71]

The forces and relations of production obey distinct historical laws. The productive forces manifest an inherent tendency to develop throughout history. The level of development is measured by their degree of productivity. The perennial impulse toward the improvement of the forces of production is grounded in and sustained by human nature and the human condition. Marx maintains that the satisfaction of biological needs is the most continuous and compelling of all human activities, and hence the prerequisite to all others:

> We must begin by stating the first premise of all human existence and, therefore, of all history, the premise, namely, that men must be in a position to live in order to be able to "make history". But life involves before everything else eating and drinking, housing, clothing and various other things. The first historical act is thus the production of the means to satisfy these needs, the production of material life itself.[72]

The human species, however, produces in a distinct manner, which distinguishes it from all other species. Men and women learn to harness natural forces to their own purposes, rationally mastering them to satisfy their requirements.[73] Human society is, fundamentally, domesticated nature, and human history is the story of its progressive domestication.[74] Accordingly, Marx suggests that an inhospitable natural environment is especially conducive to the development of industry, and hence to historical progress.[75] "Where the fruit falls from the tree into humanity's lap," explains Cohen, "there is no history because there is no need for history. History, one might say, is a substitute for nature: it occurs only when and because nature is niggardly."[76] In sum, history is the product of people's overriding interest in increasing their productive power; this interest is rooted in the facts of human nature and thus underlies social existence.

The prevailing relations of production prevail because they enable optimal increases in productivity, given the existing level of technological progress. The history of the relations of production is the history of their adaptation to the requirements of material growth. This thesis recognizes that some relations are, in the abstract, more conducive to economic growth than others. Capitalist relations are clearly more productive than feudal ones. The class system which rules is nevertheless the most suitable for maximum material progress at the time, given the stage of technological development achieved by that time. Cohen uses the following metaphor to explain: "Sports cars are faster than jeeps, but jeeps are faster on boggy land."[77]

The period of normal development of a mode of production is characterized by a state of equilibrium between property relations and the requirements of economic growth. The dominant type of property in the factors of production is precisely that which enables them to realize optimal increases in productivity. By contrast, a social contradiction becomes manifest when the dominant relations of production are no longer competent to realize the possibilities for growth which obtained under their rule. "From forms of development of the productive forces," writes Marx, "these relations turn into their fetters."[78] The increasing incompatibility between the forces and relations of production signals a period of deepening crises culminating in the triumph of new relations best qualified to preside over continued progress.

There is some ambiguity in Marx's usage of the term "fettering." One possible interpretation is that fettering refers to a situation in which the relations of production impede all further improvements in productivity.[79] This reading, however, is inconsistent with Marx's central historical claims. For example, Marx argues that capitalism's relations of production simultaneously fetter and promote the development of its productive forces. Capitalist crises typically involve violent adjustments between the relations and forces of production necessary to facilitate renewed and in fact accelerating economic growth. Moreover, the conservative implications of equating fettering with technical stagnation—for example, capitalism will not succumb to revolution until it is utterly incapable of further improving the forces—is plainly at odds with Marx's revolutionary expectations. A more plausible interpretation of fettering refers to a situation in which the dominant relations of production become suboptimal for the growth of the productive forces. An existing set of relations proves to be suboptimal when an alternative set would better develop the forces of production, even if there is some room for further material progress under the present one.[80] Thus, for example, Marx argues that capitalist private property triumphed because it was best suited to improve the productive forces once feudalism brought them to a certain stage of development.

The Nature of the Explanatory Primacy of the Productive Forces

What, then, is the theoretical connection between humanity's progressive mastery of nature and the succession of social formations in history? In the course of their development, changes in the scheme of the productive forces occasion changes in the relations of production, selecting the appropriate relations for optimal growth. This answer rescues the explanatory primacy of the productive forces from the objection that, in Marx's view, the relations of production profoundly affect technological progress, which suggests the contradictory claim that growth in productive power both explains and depends upon the relations.[81] Cohen maintains that, for Marx, the relations of production are functionally explained by the requirements of the forces:

> The effect of the relations on the forces is emphasized in our reading of the primacy [of the forces over the relations of production]. It is that effect which explains the nature of the relations, why they are as they are. The forces would not develop as they do were the relations

different, but that is *why* the relations are not different—because relations of the given kind suit the development of the forces.[82]

Accordingly, a specific set of relations of production prevails only because, and endures only during the period that, it so favors the productive forces.

This mode of analysis is a contested procedure, particularly in the social sciences. Both its defenders and detractors agree, however, that a functional *explanation* of the existence of a specific set of relations of production by the level of development of the productive forces must demonstrate, first, that this level determines which set best encourages growth, and second, that this set emerged in order to facilitate optimal growth. Any productive improvements may otherwise be explained as the unintended result of factors operating quite independently of the forces, for example, previous processes of class conflict. In other words, the validity of the functional primacy of the productive forces depends on the existence of a "feedback" mechanism whereby the forces select relations of production with the propensity to promote optimal productive development.[83]

Marx does not specify this mechanism in any rigorous fashion. Neither does Cohen, although he suggests that its presence may nevertheless be indicated, in advance of its theoretical elaboration, by the availability of suitable and sufficient empirical evidence. This evidence would reveal recurrent historical patterns between the requirements of material progress and the central features of the relations of production, patterns fine enough to suggest the hypothesis that the relations have those features because they meet the requirements of progress.[84]

We shall now argue that Marx's early historical studies marshalled evidence of this sort: They show that the forces of production have tended to develop throughout history, identify the functional requirements generated by successive levels of productive development, and reveal provocative correlations between these requirements and the rise of classes fulfilling them. These studies ascribed to the division of labor a central role in translating the imperatives of material progress into the advent of new class relations. Marx used the following analogy to illustrate:

> These social relations into which the producers enter with one another, the conditions under which they exchange their activities and participate in the whole act of production, will naturally vary according to the character of the means of production. With the invention of a new instrument of warfare, firearms, the whole internal organisation of the army necessarily changed; the relationships within which individuals can constitute an army and act as an army were transformed and the relations of different armies to one another also changed.
>
> Thus the social relations within which individuals produce, the social relations of production, change, are transformed, with the change and development of the material means of production, the productive forces.[85]

This passage postulates a causal relation between the two dimensions of the division of labor. On the one hand, the operation of any technology involves the cooperation between individuals engaged in production. This is the technical structure of the division of labor. On the other hand, the operation of any technology requires that certain individuals direct and superintend the work process, in order to secure the optimal combination of producers and productive forces. This is its authority structure. Marx suggests that any substantial change in an army's technical organization calls for a substantial change in its authority structure, which obtains and prevails precisely because it promotes its destructive power. By analogy, major advances in society's technical division of labor give rise to a need for new relations between superiors and subordinate producers, which form and endure because they enhance its productive power.[86]

This is how Marx explained the nature and direction of changes in society's form of intercourse, a term he used in his earlier works to designate what he came to call its relations of production. The level of productive development "is shown most manifestly by the degree to which the division of labour has been carried."[87] Classes rise and rule in response to material progress, whose influence on classes is mediated by advances in the technical division of labor. Thus, for example, Marx argues that the transition from feudal to capitalist relations of production in Western Europe was propelled by changes in the allocation of productive tasks witnessed in the late medieval period.[88] The expansion of trade generated a rising level of demand and promoted the accumulation of capital, thereby inducing—making both necessary and possible—a reorganization of the factors of production to increase productivity. The crucial developments took place in the towns: handicrafts, commerce, manufacture, and large scale industry constituted the main forms of productive organization which underwrote the formation of the bourgeoisie. The periodic emergence of new ways of distributing labor power in turn called for changes in the mode of directing the work process and enforcing labor discipline: the craftsmen's workshop, the merchants' trading companies and corporations, the nascent capitalists' manufactories and the modern capitalists' factories entailed specific authority relations suited to the technical requirements of running each type of producing unit.

Class relations reflected the division between mental and manual labor—that is, between the work involved in superintending production and the work involved in carrying it out.[89] Individuals who succeeded in advancing the technical division of labor to the next stage—that is, who undertook the development and organization of a new branch of production—prevailed as successive ruling fractions within the bourgeoisie.[90] The property system sustaining them comprised enforceable claims in the means of production empowering them to administer the production process. Specific relations of production obtained because they were the most conducive to economic growth, given the level of progress in technology and the organization of labor: master craftsmen directed the work of apprentices and journeymen in the small workshop; merchants subordinated craftsmen to the great trading companies and corporations; manufacturing capitalists reduced the traditional patriarchal relations between master and journeyman to the purely monetary relation between employer and semiskilled laborer obtaining in the manufactory; industrial capitalists integrated wage laborers and machines in the factory system.

Class rule entailed the adoption of institutional frameworks indispensable for the development of the productive forces: master craftsmen organized the guild system; merchants set up monopolies; manufacturers established a network of protective tariffs; industrial capitalists instituted free trade. Their very success in promoting material growth, however, rendered the existing relations of production obsolete, because the attendant mode of organizing economic activity was unsuited to the exigencies of more advanced productive forces. They thus succumbed to progress: the craft guilds confined and gave way to the operations of merchant capital; both were outstripped by manufactories, which were themselves eclipsed by the needs of large scale capitalist industry. Marx summarized the logic of this history:

> An earlier form of intercourse, which has become a fetter, is replaced by a new one corresponding to the more developed productive forces and, hence, to the advanced mode of the self-activity of individuals—a form which in its turn becomes a fetter and is then replaced by another. Since these conditions correspond at every stage to the simultaneous development of the productive forces, their history is at the same time the history of the evolving productive forces taken over by each new generation, and is therefore the history of the development of the forces of the individuals themselves.[91]

The Role of Classes

These correlations between the functional requirements produced by changes in the division of labor and the rise and fall of class formations suggest the presence of a causal mechanism operating between them. A theoretical elaboration of this mechanism raises two questions: "What activates the prospective new class? What ensures its victory?"[92] Marx's view of class interests and class struggle provides a large part of the answer. The advent of new productive forces will typically find individuals who favor introducing them into the productive sphere. They have two possible motives for doing so. On the one hand, individuals are sufficiently rational to search out and enter into property relations which facilitate material progress. The nascent ruling class in particular has cause to preserve and improve the forces, for increases in productivity underpin the size of the surplus its members anticipate for themselves. Hence they endeavor to adopt the mode of exploitation best suited to economic development. Capitalists, for example, maximize productivity in order to maximize profits. Capitalist class relations prevailed, however, because they reflected an underlying interest in productive improvements. On the other hand, individuals have an interest in employing new techniques because they reduce toil. This is particularly true among members of subordinate classes, but the possibility of a general economic advance creates a widespread hope for greater well-being amongst the population as a whole.

The existing ruling-class system, suited to a specific way of organizing and superintending the production process, eventually frustrates the possibilities for progress. The deepening contradiction between the forces and relations of production ultimately reaches an impasse. The rising class must either overturn the existing relations, or it must abandon the opportunities for further growth:

> Man never renounces what he has gained, but this does not mean that he never renounces the form of society in which he has acquired certain productive forces. On the contrary. If he is not to be deprived of the results obtained or to forfeit the fruits of civilisation, man is compelled to change all his traditional social forms as soon as the mode of commerce ceases to correspond to the productive forces acquired.[93]

Thus, although "privilege, the institution of guilds and corporations, the regulatory system of the Middle Ages" protected the development of new forces, the individuals who formed the nascent bourgeoisie would have forfeited its fruits "had [they] wished to preserve the forms under whose protection those fruits had ripened."[94] "Then," writes Marx, "begins an epoch of social revolution."[95]

Radical historical change, however, presupposes not only an interest but a capacity to execute it. How, then, does the nascent class acquire the power to transform the society as a whole? The economically most progressive sectors of the population occupy a common position with respect to the nascent productive forces, enabling them to organize as a class "for itself" in opposition to the ruling class. It is in this sense that Marx argues that the revolutionary class is the "living carrier" of the new forces of production.[96] Moreover, the type of property right in the means of production defining the rising class permits a level of productivity superior to the current type, empowering it to defeat and supplant existing class relations.[97] Class struggle thus plays an essential role in the supersession of one type of society by another. But this role is restricted to the surface of the historical process. The outcome of class struggle accounts for the nature and direction of social change: what, then, accounts for this outcome? Marx finds that the reason class struggles are settled one way and not another is the superior productive forces sustaining the victorious class.[98] The forces of production thus explain why the most productive classes or fractions of classes succeed throughout history: Those incapable of providing for the maximum development of the forces eventually lose out to those which are best qualified. Finally, there is a general stake in maintaining and improving production, so that the class best positioned to deliver it is able to attract support among other subjected classes.[99] Hence Marx claims that a rising class represents both its particular interest and a general advance for society at the time.[100]

Redefining Class

Marx's interpreters have pointed out that the widely quoted preface—the "most pregnant" statement of the technological interpretation of history—makes no mention of classes or their struggles.[101] Now, it may be that this silence is theoretically innocent, reflecting Marx's anticipation of Prussian censorship.[102] It may, however, betray a deeper problem, namely: This version of historical materialism accommodates the notion of class by changing it in ways Marx does not normally countenance. Marx's more familiar definition, corresponding to the thesis that history is class struggle, maintains that class is quintessentially a mode of exploitation. Its directing motive is the extraction of surplus labor.[103] The dominant mode of exploitation determines the pace and scope of economic development in a social formation. This thesis maintains that a person's class interest and behavior corresponds to his or her capacity and need to defend or impair the existing relations of power embodied in the mechanisms of surplus extraction. The members of the ruling class endeavor to maintain their capacity to extract additional surplus; the direct producers struggle to gain greater control over their labor power and its product. Accordingly, the class which succeeds in *appropriating* the greatest wealth, and hence prevails, is not necessarily the class with the greatest potential for improving the productive forces. Conversely, the class with the greatest productive potential may be consigned to a subordinate position.

The reason is that improving the instruments of surplus extraction need not coincide with improving the instruments of production. This view maintains a rigorous distinction between the logic of exploitation and the logic of production. Ruling-class members have an interest in preserving and enhancing their material circumstances. But the most rational way to realize their class interests is a function of the mechanisms of surplus extraction available to them. Their power depends on their capacity to reproduce these mechanisms. They thus use the wealth at their disposal to maintain and improve them. This use of wealth, however, may be quite incompatible with its use to maintain and improve the forces of production. To the extent that the means of exploitation diverge from the means of production, class systems systematically block productive development.

The view that history is the growth of human productive power, in contrast, reduces the logic of exploitation to the logic of production, yielding a very different definition of class. On this account, class is not, or not essentially, a mode of surplus extraction. Rather, it is a mode of optimizing society's productive potential; systems of exploitation are more fundamentally systems of allocating labor power and productive resources to promote economic growth. Hence Marx defines the relations of production as "forms of development of the productive forces. . . ."[104] The network of ownership rights denotes the authority structure within productive organizations, and the authority structure in turn reflects the functional requirements of superintending the work process, given the level of technological growth achieved at the time. A ruling class does not, therefore, preside over production because it rules; it rules because it presides over production. Some authority structures have greater productive potential than others; a specific authority structure obtains because it secures the most appropriate way of combining the factors of production to achieve the maximum development of the productive forces.

This thesis suggests an instrumental notion of class interest and behavior. In this view, a class's desire to appropriate the maximum surplus normally results in a desire to produce it. Classes can be expected to develop the mode of exploitation with the greatest productive potential because the most rational way to maximize surplus appropriation is to maximize productivity, and human beings can be expected to be somewhat rational. The struggle for supremacy between a ruling and a rising class is therefore not a clash between two appropriating classes struggling to secure dominance of a different mode of surplus extraction. Rather, it is in essence an antagonism over different ways of deploying the forces of production to achieve optimal material progress. Exploiters come to occupy the position they do because their mode of exploitation is the most productive, and they maintain their position only during the historical interval that their economic contribution is superior. Rival classes which fail to maximize productive development will be defeated by those who succeeded in doing so. "The class which rules through a period," explains Cohen, "or emerges triumphant after epochal conflict, is the class best suited, most able and disposed, to preside over the development of the productive forces at the given time."[105] The outcome of any qualitative social transformation in history is therefore a foregone conclusion: the new class relations facilitate the highest possible rate of material development, consonant with the available productive forces.

The validity of these two versions of historical materialism will now be evaluated in a historical study of the feudal mode of production and its transition to the capitalist mode of production in Western Europe. Specifically, we now seek to assess which version of historical materialism can better explain: (a) the nature of class relations and struggles in a particular historical context; (b) the main features of economic development; (c) the configuration of a crisis complex within a mode of production; and (d) the process of transition to a qualitatively new mode.

NOTES

1. Marx, *Manifesto of the Communist Party*, Vol. 6 of *Collected Works*, p. 482. (Hereafter *CW*.)
2. Anthony Giddens, *The Class Structure of the Advanced Societies*, pp. 91–92.
3. See Draper, Vol. 1 of *Karl Marx's Theory of Revolution*, p. 14–17.
4. Marx, *Manifesto of the Communist Party*, *CW* 6:487. For a "laundry list" of Marx's variable use of the term, see Draper, *Karl Marx's Theory of Revolution*, 1:17.
5. Marx, Vol. 3 of *Capital*, p. 791. See also Marx, *Capital* 1:209 and 2:36–37.
6. See, for example, Marx, *Capital* 1:226–33, 505. Marx mentions three other types of society: primitive communism, a term he uses to designate the earliest forms of human society, which were typically albeit not necessarily egalitarian (see, for example, Marx, *The German Ideology*, *CW* 5:32–33); the "Asiatic" form of Society, in which the state directly appropriated, through taxation, surplus labor from immediate producers who possessed the land they worked (see for example, Marx, *Capital* 3:791); and the anticipated socialist-communist society, which experiences a continuous revolution toward greater social equality (see, for example, Marx, *Critique of the Gotha Program*, in *The Marx-Engels Reader*, pp. 529–31). For a more exhaustive discussion of possible types of class relations, see G. A. Cohen, *Karl Marx's Theory of History*, pp. 34–35, 63–69.
7. Giddens, *The Class Structure of the Advanced Societies*, p. 29. See Marx, *The German Ideology*, *CW* 5:76–77, 78, 80; and *The Eighteenth Brumaire of Louis Bonaparte*, *CW* 11:187.
8. Letter to Conrad Schmidt, 5 August 1890, in *Selected Correspondence*, p. 393.
9. Marx, *The Poverty of Philosophy*, *CW* 6:197.
10. Marx, *Capital* 3:885.
11. Marx, *Manifesto of the Communist Party*, *CW* 6:482–85.
12. Marx, *The German Ideology*, *CW* 5:76–77, 83.
13. Marx, *Manifesto of the Communist Party*, *CW* 6:491–92.
14. Marx, *The German Ideology*, *CW* 5:76–77.

15. "In Marxist usage," writes Perry Anderson, "the purport of the concept of social formation . . . is to underline the plurality and heterogeneity of possible modes of production within any given historical and social totality. . . . Social formations . . . are . . . concrete combinations of different modes of production, organized under the dominance of one of them." Anderson, *Passages From Antiquity to Feudalism*, p. 22, n. 6.

16. Marx, *The German Ideology*, *CW* 5:83.

17. Cobban, *The Social Interpretation of the French Revolution*, pp. 22–23.

18. Marx, Letter to Engels, 27 July 1854, *CW* 39:474.

19. Marx, *The German Ideology*, *CW* 5:34.

20. Ibid., p. 78. Engels writes that "the revolution of the bourgeoisie abolished estates and their privileges. Bourgeois society knows only classes." Note to the German Edition (1885) of Marx's *The Poverty of Philosophy*, *CW* 6:212.

21. Hence M. I. Finley dismisses the usefulness of the Marxian concept of class for the historian of classical antiquity, but only because he first (mis)construes this concept as a narrowly economic phenomenon, suitable only for the analysis of modern capitalist societies. M. I. Finley, *The Ancient Economy* (Berkeley: University of California Press, 1973), pp. 49–50.

22. Marx, *Capital* 3:790–91.

23. Hilton, *Bond Men Made Free*, pp. 44–55; Hilton, "Feudalism in Europe," pp. 86–87.

24. Ellen Meiksins Wood and Neal Wood, *Class Ideology and Ancient Political Theory*, p. 61.

25. Ibid., p. 53.

26. *The Poverty of Philosophy*, *CW* 6:221; *The Eighteenth Brumaire*, *CW* 11:187.

27. G. A. Cohen, *Karl Marx's Theory of History*, p. 73 and n.

28. Ibid.

29. Ibid., p. 76. See also Anderson, *Arguments Within English Marxism*, pp. 40, 43.

30. Thompson, "Eighteenth Century English Society," p. 142.

31. Anderson, *Arguments Within English Marxism*, p. 55. Emphasis added.

32. Ellen Meiksins Wood, "The Politics of Theory and the Concept of Class," pp. 50–51.

33. Ibid., p. 63.

34. G. A. Cohen, *Karl Marx's Theory of History*, p. 74.

35. Thompson, "Eighteenth Century English Society," p. 149. See

also Thompson, *The Making of the English Working Class*, pp. 9–11; Marx, *The German Ideology*, *CW* 5:76–77, 78, 80.

36. Anderson, *Arguments Within English Marxism*, p. 43.

37. See Edward Andrew, "Class in Itself and Class Against Capital," pp. 577–84.

38. Marx, *CW* 6:221.

39. Marx, *CW* 11:187.

40. Marx, *The Eighteenth Brumaire*, *CW* 11:188, 189–190.

41. These dynamics will be examined in some detail below, in chapters 3 and 5.

42. Marx, *The Eighteenth Brumaire*, *CW* 11:187. See also Marx, *The Class Struggles in France*, *CW* 10:134.

43. See Marx, *The Class Struggles in France*, *CW* 10:80; and *The Eighteenth Brumaire*, *CW* 11:188, 193.

44. Marx points out that Louis Napoleon was not simply a peasant phenomenon. He was supported by sizeable numbers in other classes, albeit for their own reasons. What permitted Napoleon to assume power, Marx argues, is precisely the fact that the emperor meant different things to each of the major contending classes. Marx decodes the *idées napoléoniennes* in terms of the class-differential ways in which they were interpreted. Just as he shows that class formation and consciousness are not simply expressions of class location, he also shows that the same ideas simultaneously pointed to distinct conclusions for various classes. The peasants appropriated the ruling ideas in their own ways, fashioning out of them a distinctive response to their predicament. See Marx, *The Class Struggles in France*, *CW* 10:80–81, 85; *The Eighteenth Brumaire*, *CW* 11:193–96. Similarly, medieval peasants interpreted the ruling religious ideas in their own ways, appropriating the symbolism of the poverty of Jesus of Nazareth as their own, and using it to challenge the authority of the feudal ruling class. See Hilton, *Bond Men Made Free*, pp. 97–109.

45 Wood, "The Politics of Theory and the Concept of Class," p. 64.

46. See, for example, Marx, *The German Ideology*, *CW* 5:78–79.

47. See G. A. Cohen, "Forces and Relations of Production," pp. 19–21.

48. Jon Elster, *Making Sense of Marx*, p. 318.

49. Marx, *Capital* 3:793–96. This issue is examined more fully below in Chapter 3.

50. Ibid., pp. 790–91.

51. See Hilton, "A Crisis of Feudalism," in *The Brenner Debate*, ed. Aston and Philpin, pp. 119–37.

52. This is Marx's explanation for the tendency of the rate of profit

to fall in capitalist economies. See *Capital* 1:289 and 3:212–13, 264–65.

53. Marx, *Capital* 3:796. See also Hilton, "A Crisis of Feudalism," in *The Brenner Debate*, ed. Aston and Philpin, pp. 128–31.

54. Anderson, *Lineages of the Absolutist State*, pp. 15–42.

55. See Anderson, *Passages*, p. 204.

56. These twin claims—that ruling classes rule because they are best for (or facilitate) optimal productive development, and that they emerge triumphant precisely because they thus favor material progress—are advanced by the thesis ascribing explanatory primacy to the forces of production. These claims will be examined in the following section of this chapter.

57. Marx, *CW* 6:482.

58. Marx, *The Poverty of Philosophy*, *CW* 6:211.

59. Marx, *Manifesto of the Communist Party*, *CW* 6:482.

60. See Miller, *Analyzing Marx*, pp. 172–73, 174–75, 205–20. See also Levine and Wright, "Rationality and Class Struggle," pp. 47–68; Ellen Meiksins Wood, "Marxism and the Course of History," pp. 95–107.

61. G. A. Cohen, *Karl Marx's Theory of History*, pp. 134–74.

62. See Marx, *Capital* 1:173–80.

63. G. A. Cohen has provided an excellent account of Marx's understanding of the forces of production and their constituent elements. *Karl Marx's Theory of History*, pp. 28–62.

64. Thus, it is only the *written* history of all hitherto existing society which is the history of class struggles. See the note Engels appended to the *Communist Manifesto*, *CW* 6:482. And this "prehistory" of human society comes to a close with the dissolution of class antagonisms heralded by the anticipated socialist transformation. See Marx's preface to *A Contribution to the Critique of Political Economy*, in *The Marx-Engels Reader*, p. 5.

65. Shaw places the division of labor within the relations of production. See Shaw, *Marx's Theory of History*, pp. 30–31. McMurtry, in contrast, locates the division of labor within the productive forces. See McMurtry, *The Structure of Marx's World-View*, pp. 72–73. G. A. Cohen's view is that the division of labor constitutes a distinct category, denoting relationships which are neither part of the relations nor the forces of production. G. A. Cohen, *Karl Marx's Theory of History*, pp. 111–14.

66. Marx, *The German Ideology*, *CW* 5:32–33, 44–45, 46, 63–74, 77–78, 80, 436–37; Marx, *Capital* 1:313–14, 341, 399, 476; and Marx, *Critique of the Gotha Program*, in *The Marx-Engels Reader*, p. 531. See also Robert Brenner, "Marx's First Model of the Transition to Capitalism,"

in *Marx en Perspective*, ed. Chavance pp. 205–06, 217–18; Kolakowski, in Vol. 1 of *Main Currents of Marxism*, pp. 337–38.

67. Marx, *The German Ideology*, *CW* 5:43. Marx sometimes uses the terms "mode of cooperation" and "mode of production" interchangeably. This particular use of the term "mode of production," however, must be distinguished from its more common usage to identify global combinations of the relations and forces of production in history, for example, the capitalist mode of production.

68. Marx, *Capital* 1:308–12.

69. Marx, *The German Ideology*, *CW* 5:32–35, 50–51, 64–74; Marx, *Capital* 1:332–34. Cf. G. A. Cohen, *Karl Marx's Theory of History*, pp. 298–302.

70. Marx, *The German Ideology*, *CW* 5:68–72. And Marx, *Manifesto of the Communist Party*, *CW* 6:485.

71. Marx, *The German Ideology*, *CW* 5:71–72. Also, Marx, *The Poverty of Philosophy*, *CW* 6:185–187. And, Marx, *Capital* 1:318–20, 329–30, 344, 347.

72. Marx, *The German Ideology*, *CW* 5:41–42. See also Marx, Letter to Kugelmann, 11 July 1868, in *Selected Correspondence*, p. 196.

73. Marx, *Capital* 1:174, 179.

74. Marx, *Economic and Philosophic Manuscripts of 1844*, *CW* 3:302–303; *Grundrisse*, pp. 487–488.

75. Marx, *Capital* 1:481.

76. G. A. Cohen, "Restrictive and Inclusive Historical Materialism," in *Marx en Perspective*, ed. Chavance, p. 55.

77. G. A. Cohen, *Karl Marx's Theory of History*, p. 171. See also G. A. Cohen, "Reply to Four Critics," p. 199.

78. Marx, preface to *A Contribution to the Critique of Political Economy*, in *The Marx-Engels Reader*, pp. 4–5.

79. See, for example, Kolakowski, *Main Currents in Marxism* 1:301, 302, 375.

80. Miller, *Analyzing Marx*, pp. 177–78; Elster, *Making Sense of Marx*, pp. 258–63. Elster suggests a third interpretation of fettering: viz., a situation in which the relations of production frustrate the optimal *use* rather than the optimal development of the productive forces. Ibid., pp. 263–67. He maintains, however, that development fettering "is at the core of historical materialism." Ibid., p. 259.

81. See Kolakowski, *Main Currents of Marxism* 1:368–69, 2:208.

82. G. A. Cohen, *Karl Marx's Theory of History*, p. 161. See also G. A. Cohen, "Reply to Four Critics," p. 199.

83. See, for example, Philippe van Parijs, "Marxism's Central Puzzle," in *After Marx*, ed. Terrence Ball and James Farr, pp. 88–104. See

also G. A. Cohen, "Reply to Four Critics," pp. 201–06; Elster, *Making Sense of Marx*, pp. 268–69; Rigby, *Marxism and History*, pp. 84–91. We shall not address the voluminous literature on the validity of functional explanations in the social sciences. G. A. Cohen has offered a sophisticated and lucid defense of functional explanations in Marxism. See G. A. Cohen, *Karl Marx's Theory of History*, pp. 249–92. Cohen subsequently refined his views. See Cohen, "Functional Explanation, Consequence Explanation and Marxism," pp. 27–56. For doubts regarding the validity of functional Marxism, see the debate in *Theory and Society* 11 (July 1982).

84. G. A. Cohen, *Karl Marx's Theory of History*, pp. 285–87.

85. Marx, *Wage Labor and Capital*, *CW* 9:211–12. Marx underscored the significance of this analogy in improving his understanding of the primacy of the forces over the relations of production. See Marx's Letter to Engels, 25 September 1857, *CW* 40:186–87. I owe this point to G. A. Cohen. See *Karl Marx's Theory of History*, p. 146, n. 1.

86. Cf. G. A. Cohen, *Karl Marx's Theory of History*, p. 166. To be sure, Marx's later works, which tend to ascribe explanatory primacy to class, reverse the causal relationship between authority relations and the technical division of labor. In these works, Marx maintains that authority relations serve the purpose of maximizing exploitation, and that this aim may result in an inefficient division of labor. See, for example, *Capital* 1:313–15, 394–400.

87. Marx, *The German Ideology*, *CW* 5:32.

88. The following interpretation of Marx's account of the transition from feudalism to capitalism is distilled primarily from: Marx, *The German Ideology*, *CW* 5:32–35, 63–74; *The Poverty of Philosophy*, *CW* 6:185–87; *Manifesto of the Communist Party*, *CW* 6:485–489. See also Brenner, "Marx's First Model of the Transition to Capitalism," in *Marx en Perspective*, ed. Chavance, pp. 203–30.

89. Marx, *The German Ideology*, *CW* 5:32, 44–45, 46.

90. Ibid., pp. 76–77. See also Marx, *Manifesto of the Communist Party*, *CW* 6:486.

91. Marx, *The German Ideology*, *CW* 5:82. See also Marx, *Manifesto of the Commuisty Party*, *CW* 6:489.

92. G. A. Cohen, "Forces and Relations of Production," p. 22.

93. Letter to Annenkov, 28 December 1846, *CW* 38:96–97.

94. Ibid., p. 97.

95. Marx, preface to *A Contribution to the Critique of Political Economy*, in *The Marx-Engels Reader*, p. 5.

96. Marx, *The Poverty of Philosophy*, *CW* 6:211; *Grundrisse*, p. 541.

97. G. A. Cohen, *Karl Marx's Theory of History*, pp. 207–08.

98. Ibid., pp. 148–49.
99. Ibid., p. 292. See Engels, *Socialism: Utopian and Scientific*, in *The Marx-Engels Reader*, pp. 684–685.
100. Marx, *The German Ideology*, *CW* 6:60–61; Marx, "The Bourgeoisie and the Counter-Revolution," *CW* 8:161.
101. Eric J. Hobsbawm, Introduction to Karl Marx, *Pre-Capitalist Economic Formations*, tr. Jack Cohen (New York: International Publishers, 1964), p. 11.
102. Printz, "Background and Ulterior Motives of Marx's Preface of 1859," pp. 437–50.
103. See Marx, *Capital* 1:313–15, 398–400.
104. Marx, preface to *A Contribution to the Critique of Political Economy*, in *The Marx-Engels Reader*, p. 4.
105. G. A. Cohen, *Karl Marx's Theory of History*, p. 149.

3

The Feudal Mode of Production

What is the internal dynamic which explains feudalism's economic development and decline? The arguments which frame the discussion may be provisionally stated thus: An examination of medieval history provides striking confirmation of the Marxian thesis that a mode of production is structured in terms of class struggle. The direct clash of class interests over the allocation of labor and its product constituted the prime mover of the feudal economy, determining its characteristic trends. The conflict between lords and peasants propelled the development of the productive forces. Economic expansion was marked, but class relations did not permit anything like optimal productivity increases, given the existing level of technological progress. Contradictions inherent in the feudal system of exploitation eventually precipitated a crisis which convulsed the mode of production as a whole. This crisis, however, was not one in which a new set of productive forces burst through the existing relations of production, pointing toward an epochal historical transition. Rather, the feudal crisis complex took the form of a dramatic contraction of the technical infrastructure within the dominant class relations, severely crippling material life. Peasant revolts—"as natural to the seigneurial regime as strikes . . . are to large-scale capitalism," wrote Marc Bloch[1]—played the central role in bringing feudal exploitation to an end. The objectives of rebellious peasants, however, were normally confined to resisting seigneurial encroachments; its conditions of existence prevented the peasantry from becoming an alternative ruling class. This argument raises suspicions concerning the Marxian thesis that the logic of class struggle inherent in a mode of production, grounded in the relationship of exploitation, gives rise to a class with the capacity and the interest to reorganize society as a whole.

The study of the feudal mode of production, however, lends little support to the thesis that the nature of a society's relations of production is explained by the level of development of its productive forces. Indeed, few historians of the medieval period have found this thesis useful; no Marxist historian has put it to work, to any significant extent, in a study of the feudal economy and society. G. A. Cohen's philosophical defense of the primacy of the productive forces does, to be sure, cite one text adhering to a technological interpretation of feudal development.[2] He admits, however, that its central argument has been "subjected to severe and convincing criticism. . . . "[3] It may be, of course, that historical studies which do not explicitly ascribe causal primacy to productive development are nevertheless consonant with it. We shall argue, on the contrary, that the historical record is plainly incompatible with this thesis. The paucity of both historical studies and historical evidence supporting the technological reading of historical materialism is surely one of the most telling criticisms against it.

Cohen is well aware that precapitalist modes of production present a problem for his defense of Marx's theory of history.[4] In contrast to capitalist relations of production, Marx argued, precapitalist relations were essentially conservative: they made limited contributions to productive development. How, then, can they be explained in terms of their propensity to promote material progress? Cohen answers that precapitalist relations of production were the most suitable relations for economic growth at the time when they prevailed, given the level of technological development reached by that time.[5] The class which ruled, he maintains, ruled precisely because it was best able and disposed to develop the productive forces of this age.[6] We shall argue, however, that the nature of feudal class relations not only constrained economic growth, it blocked the employment of productive methods and implements already known and available to medieval producers.[7] Indeed, Marx's account of the feudal dynamic shows that the contending classes influenced the economy in a way that turns Cohen's thesis upside down. For it is the class which prevailed and ruled, the lords that impeded progress; the subordinate class, the peasants, were primarily responsible for the material progress witnessed in medieval Europe. The forces of production, in other words, would have been better served had the peasantry not been subjugated to feudal rule.

The Marxian thesis that class struggle constitutes the prime mover of the feudal mode of production does not stand uncontested among historians. The principal competing paradigm is one which assigns primary responsibility for changes in the medieval economy to the inexorable movements of rising and falling population. The aim of this paradigm, in the words of two of its leading exponents, is "to relate periodic movements or economic fluctuations . . . to concomitant demographic changes . . . over time."[8] These historians do not ignore the significance of class relations when interpreting the medieval economy and society. Rather, they explain changes in class relations in terms of demographic trends.[9]

The elemental imperatives of human biology and the inclemency of the natural environment form a central focus of the demographic thesis. Despite this similarity with the technological interpretation of historical materialism, however, their explanations are ultimately incompatible. For the demographic thesis argues that population pressures did not induce (otherwise rational) individuals to increase productivity. Quite the contrary, medieval population growth normally culminated in demographic collapse—precipitous drops in population due to starvation and pestilence.

The fundamental presupposition of the demographic paradigm is a traditional economy inherently incapable of making more than limited contributions to productive development.[10] Given this economic situation, the feudal dynamic can be accurately interpreted in terms of the impact of a natural tendency for the population to increase on a given supply of land.

First, shifts in the relative fortunes of the contending classes, that is, in the economic conditions of existence of lords and peasants, can primarily be understood as the result of shifts in the land to labor ratio. Thus, on the one hand, long and lengthening queues of peasant families seeking land tended to strengthen the hand of the nobility, enabling them to employ the mechanisms of surplus extraction at their command to increase their demands on the peasantry. On the other hand, demographic decline would empower the peasants to loosen the grip of aristocratic domination, as the lords competed for an ever scarcer supply of labor.[11]

Second, the demographic paradigm provides a cogent explanation of the feudal crisis complex: Given the economy's inability to make improvements in agricultural production, the rising pressure of population growth on the land led to a fall in average yields due to the declining fertility of the soil and the occupation of ever more marginal terrain. Against the background of this increasingly precarious ecological imbalance, demographic expansion eventually tipped the scale to overpopulation. The resulting crisis assumed its characteristic expression in a crisis of subsistence and demographic collapse.[12] This theory thus accounts for the fate of the peasantry at the close of the Middle Ages: if the sufferings of the peasants had been terrible during the crisis, reconstruction, when it came, witnessed a golden age for the European cultivator.

The demographic and Marxian paradigms are in agreement concerning the long-term trends of the feudal economy. Moreover, the concentration on the land to labor ratio has provided historians with an internally consistent and compelling explanation of these trends and, more specifically, of the dynamics of the feudal crisis complex. Nevertheless, Marxian class analysis exposes two telling weaknesses in demographic interpretations. First, this approach depends upon an assumption for which it cannot systematically account: namely, the technological stagnation of medieval society.[13] Needless to say, it is not the *fact* of the feudal economy's inertia that is in dispute here, but its explanation. M. M. Postan, accurately enough, links the paucity of technical innovation to the lack of investment. But this answer only pushes the question back one step: Why was the flow of investment into agricultural improvement so sluggish? At this point, the demographic historians falter. They appeal to the cultural horizons of medieval Europe, that is, to the normative preferences of the lords and the wealthier peasants.[14] Why this particular set of preferences prevailed during this period is left unexplained. The strength of the Marxian approach, by contrast, lies precisely in the fact that it systematically links the scale of values of the contending classes to the imperatives of the class struggle.[15] Thus, for example, each of the normative preferences M. M. Postan and John Hatcher adduced to explain landlord investments—"a gentleman's or a baron's standing in his region . . . ; the following he was able to recruit and the power he could mobilize . . . ; his ability to provide for daughters or to form family alliances, and even to ensure salvation by religious or charitable endowments"[16]—can be referred back to the imperatives of maintaining the conditions of feudal class rule.[17]

The Marxian analysis explains the impact of population trends in terms of the patterns of medieval investment and accumulation, and the latter, in turn, are accounted for by the imperatives inherent in the nature of the feudal class relation. Accordingly, Marx argued that "every special historic mode of production has its own special laws of population, historically valid within its limits alone."[18]

This argument leads us to the second shortcoming of the demographic approach: It cannot explain the transition from feudalism to capitalism.[19] This is the question Marxian theory is especially interested in answering: Why does population growth cease to come up against "Malthusian blockages" (Le Roy Ladurie's term) in England towards the end of the seventeenth century and in France towards the end of the eighteenth? Clearly, because the capitalist economy establishes a close, if imperfect, link between the predominant uses of material resources and the requirements of productive development. This link, however, cannot, or not principally, be explained as the result of the fortuitous rise of a new scale of values, but rather as the consequence of the emergence of class relationships that make productive development essential to the preservation of capitalist rule.

CLASS STRUCTURE

The analysis of feudalism's economic development requires a study of the physiognomy of medieval rural society. In sharp contrast to capitalist wealth, which takes the form of commodities, feudal wealth assumed the form of land. Feudal class struggle was based in the countryside. The economy of the Middle Ages was primarily agricultural, and its agriculture was in the main arable. Labor and its products were as a rule retained within the rural domestic economy of lords and peasants. Industry and agriculture did not form specialized spheres of production, separated in town and country; they were interwoven into rural life.[20] Craftsmen were integral members of peasant communities, performing essential ancillary functions for agricultural production. Ironsmiths, for example, were a focal point in the village, typically possessing some land as well as a workshop.[21] Medieval cities contained a small proportion of the population, and the character of their economic structure was, on the whole, dependent upon and sustained by the social configuration and rhythm of agrarian production.[22] The nature of urban industry was shaped by the composition of effective rural demand—that is, by the mix of aristocratic demand for luxury products and peasant demand for producer and consumer goods—and thus by the balance of class relations on the land.[23] More importantly, the very potential for urban industrial development depended upon the possibility of diverting productive resources, especially labor, from the countryside to the city, and thus upon the level of productive development achieved by the agrarian economy.[24] The subordination of the country to the town's economy and its transformation into "agriculture"—that is, into a specialized branch of the social division of labor—is the accomplishment of the capitalist mode of production. This transformation, however, presupposed a revolution in agricultural relations of production.[25]

The differentia distinguishing feudalism as a historically specific mode of production was the manor or seigneurie. Its internal structure constituted the society's system of surplus extraction: The manor comprised a set of effective property rights in the means of production that enabled the nobility to command and thus exploit the labor of the peasantry. Its study thus reveals both the nature of feudal class relations and the possibilities they opened for economic development. The starting point of this study is an examination of its constituent classes: lords and serfs.

The economic basis of the manor, indeed of feudal society as a whole, was peasant agriculture and its ancillary crafts. Its product provided the necessary material support for the whole superstructure of aristocracy, church, towns, and state. What, then, was the internal composition of the peasantry as a class? Its basic component was the individual holding of the peasant family. The household economy comprised the means of production of the family's livelihood: Mainly, rights of access to the cultivable lands for sown crops, which were separately appropriated; access to the village commons, encompassing primarily grazing lands for animals; and access to woods for gathering timber used for building and fuel. Peasant holdings were reproduced by the family's own labor force. The typical holding formed a natural economic cell in the sense that the material conditions of its continued existence—the labor of the family and its product—were directly replaced out of the household economy itself.[26] The characteristic type of peasant holding, characteristic in the sense that it represented the central core of the peasantry as a class, not necessarily the majority of households, was sufficiently large, and enjoyed sufficient rights in its various common appurtenances to make it a viable economic unit. This means that the holding was large enough to permit the household to be self-subsistent, making "it unnecessary for the family to depend on regular employment for wages, yet not so large as to permit the family to live wholly on the proceeds of rents or to enable it to work its holding entirely or mainly by hired labor."[27]

The peasant family did not have full ownership of the fields it cultivated, nor did the village community exercise full proprietary rights over the commons. "Both were said to be 'held' of the lord, which meant that as landowner he had a superior right over them, recognised by dues owed to him, and capable in certain circumstances of overriding the concurrent rights of the individual cultivators and of the community."[28] Feudal property rights were scalar, specifying various terms of access to the same piece of land and differentiated only by degree.[29] The peasant family "possessed" its holding, and although the terms of tenure varied, particularly between villein and free, its property claims, usually supported by custom, could be defended in the manor's court or, if the situation permitted, in the public court.[30] The peasant's relationship to the means of production is thus very different from that of the slave or the modern proletarian. Unlike slaves and wage laborers, who work under alien conditions of production, peasants work independently.[31] Peasants had traditionally lived on the product of the lands they cultivated on their own account "from time immemorial, before falling under the domination of a lord who used his power to establish legal ownership of [them]."[32]

The significance of this fact emerges when we recall that peasant holdings were not economically autonomous units. They were embedded within village communities which tightly regulated the production process. The economic basis of the characteristic village was the practice of farming in common or open fields:

> First, the arable and meadow is divided into strips among the cultivators, each of whom may occupy a number of strips scattered about the fields. Secondly, both arable and meadow are thrown open for common pasturing by the stock of all the commoners after harvest and in fallow seasons. In the arable fields this means necessarily that some rules about cropping are observed so that spring and winter sown crops may be grown in separate fields or furlongs. Thirdly, there is common pasturage and waste, where cultivators of strips enjoy the rights to graze stock and gather timber, peat and other commodities. . . . Fourthly, the ordering of these activities is regulated by an assembly of cultivators—the manorial court . . . or, where more than one manor was present in a township, a village meeting.[33]

The continuous coordination of tasks required to operate this agricultural system formed the practical basis of collective village action and strength.[34] It created a dense nexus of ties, rights and obligations that wove the peasants into a cohesive social force. It is necessary to draw a distinction, however, between the peasantry's place in the scheme of the productive forces and its place in the network of ownership relations. On the one hand, the patterns of land use and the operation of the existing agricultural technology gave rise to a mode of cooperation among villagers which equipped them with the capacity for concerted action.[35] On the other hand, the aim of the peasants' struggle as a *class* was derived from their place in the feudal property system. The experiential basis from which they evolved a consciousness of their common identity, the sense of the distinctive interests they shared, was formed by repeated confrontations with the lords over the appropriation of their labor power and its product. To be sure, there were internal inequalities within the village community, primarily "between the owners of plough teams and those who had to hire themselves out to live."[36] Yet the divisive potential of this stratification was always strictly limited by the imperative of defending the interests of the village as a whole against seigneurial encroachments.[37] In short, the main impetus behind sustained peasant solidarity was the necessity of class struggle. The best evidence for this argument, as we shall see, is that when manorial institutions lost their vigor, the raison d'être of the village community dissolved, the economic divisions within the peasantry became progressively more pronounced, and ultimately destroyed the peasants' capacity to act as a class.

The context of feudal class struggle was the institution of landlordship. This institution had a dual structure: As a fief, it established the internal cohesion of the aristocracy as a class; as a manor, it empowered the lords to extract an economic surplus from the peasantry. The lordship was created by the fusion of parcellized sovereignty and scalar property that distinguished the feudal regime.[38] The noble, like the peasant, did not enjoy full ownership rights over his estates. Rather, the estate was held in "fief"—hence the term feudalism—a conditional tenancy which was simultaneously the component cell of medieval government. The lord's estate became the state:[39] "an amalgam of property and sovereignty, in which the partial nature of the one was matched by the private character of the other; conditional tenure was structurally linked to individual jurisdiction."[40] The fief established a network of vertical ties and obligations sometimes described by the term "vassalage," which, despite deep internal cleavages of power and wealth, wove the aristocracy into a single unit of social intercourse—"an association against a subjected producing class," wrote Marx.[41]

Landlordship conferred wealth and power by virtue of investing the lord's tenancy with jursidictional and administrative authority over dependent peasant cultivators. This was the economic basis of lordship—the manor. Its social physiognomy specified the distinctive nature of the relationship between nobles and peasants. The representative manor was divided between the lord's home farm, or demesne, and the holdings let out to peasant tenants. The direct producers typically divided their labor time between their plots and the lord's fields. In this context, wrote Marx, "rent and surplus-value are identical. Rent, not profit, is the form . . . through which unpaid surplus-labour expresses itself."[42] The territorial division comprising the manor yielded the lord a dual source of revenue: rent in the form of unpaid labor services on his demesne, and rent in kind or money from the peasants' holdings. The essential element of this bilateral division was that the two constituents of land and income were tightly interwoven. "In an 'ideal' manor the demesne would be of a size capable of being served by its tenants, while the land in tenancy would be large enough and the tenants numerous enough to provide the demesne with the labor it required."[43]

The link binding demesne with tenants was established by the feudal system of exploitation. Marx writes: "The direct producer . . . is to be found here in possession of his own means of production, the necessary material labour conditions required for the realisation of his labour and the production of his means of subsistence."[44] Medieval peasant villagers were quite capable, in economic terms, of reproducing their conditions of life without the intervention of any ruling class. Surplus labor was therefore necessarily extracted from them "by other than economic pressure."[45] Accordingly, the property system took the form of "a direct relation of lordship and servitude, so that the direct producer is not free."[46] The lord was empowered to control the labor of the peasants by virtue of his superior right to make binding decisions regarding the disposition of their persons and lands.

This juridical relationship specified the characteristic form of labor power in the feudal mode of production—serfdom. The term is plagued by controversy, but it is sufficient for our purposes to adopt Marx's own definition: a "condition of personal dependence . . . a lack of personal freedom, no matter to what extent, and being tied to the soil as its accessory, bondage in the true sense of the word."[47] The main effect of serfdom "was to ensure that peasant families were kept on the holdings, and to guarantee for the lord the payment of rent and the performance of services."[48] It should be emphasized, however, that the various rules of dependence meant that ground rent, whether in labor, kind, or money was not the sole or even the main form in which surplus was appropriated. The lack of freedom carried a bewildering number of other economic burdens: Seigneurial jurisdiction gave the lord the right of command (the *ban*) which permitted him to compel tenants to use, and pay for, his mills, ovens, or wine presses; it entitled him to restrict the mobility of the peasants, compelling them to purchase permission to move or marry outside the manor; and it empowered him to control the disposition of peasant lands, forcing them to buy licenses for transactions involving lease or sale, and subjecting them to payments for admission to a holding and upon the death of the tenant. Peasants were also assessed fines for a wide range of offenses they might commit in contravention of the lord's right. Finally, there was the seigneurial tax or tallage, particularly onerous by virtue of being arbitrary.

The class relationship between lords and peasants established the distinctive historical identity of the feudal mode of production. We now turn to examine the impact of this relationship on the development of the productive forces.

THE FEUDAL DYNAMIC

Class struggle constitutes the dynamic regulating a society's long-term economic trends. Productive development depends upon the size and use of socially produced wealth. Productivity increases are achieved by applying economic resources to improving society's productive forces. The specific way in which individuals use their resources, however, is governed by imperatives inherent in the class system, not by the requirements of economic growth. The class positions in which people find themselves specify their terms of access to labor power and the means of production. The nature of these terms, which are contested in class struggles, determines the main avenues available to them to improve their material circumstances and thus conditions the way they use the resources at their disposal. Accordingly, the pace of economic growth depends upon the extent to which their class position induces individuals to improve their circumstances by making productive investments.

The lords sought to protect their power to appropriate an economic surplus from the dependent peasant cultivators, both against rival lords and against the subjected producing class. The peasants, on the other hand, endeavored to retain the whole of their labor and its product within the household economy. Thus, the main features of peasant class consciousness were "a deeply rooted sense of family property rights in the peasant holding, . . . [and] the consequential attitude that the family should be able to devote all of its labor to the cultivation and maintenance of the holding."[49] Accordingly, whereas the lords sought to reduce the peasantry to the conditions of villein tenure, the peasants struggled to restrict their obligations to those corresponding to common law free tenure.[50] It is worth emphasizing that labor rent was not necessarily the essential focus of medieval class struggle; nor can the commutation of labor services therefore be equated with the end of the feudal epoch. The central freedom sought by peasants was the secure right to their lands and persons—for example, to move, to dispose of their property, to marry and form a family, to bequeath or inherit lands and livestock, and so on—in short, freedom from the main weight of servile disabilities. To be sure, the peasants found labor rent on the lord's demesne particularly oppressive, for it struck at the very root of their attempt to dispose of their and their family's labor power. But it was a comparatively poor source of revenue for the lords as well: compulsory labor services were grudgingly and thus badly performed and close supervision and control were difficult to obtain.[51] Hence, throughout the medieval West, there was on balance a general evolution away from labor rent toward rents in kind and money, and from ground rent as a whole toward seigneurial taxation and the profits of jurisdiction.[52]

What, then, was the impact of feudal class struggle on productive development? We shall examine the economic functions of the contending classes in turn, beginning with the nobles. The lords' main contributions to economic growth were by-products of their efforts to maximize the appropriation of an economic surplus from the peasantry. Their command over superior productive resources made possible the use of the water mill, one of the most significant technical innovations of the Middle Ages.[53] Its introduction armed the lords with one of the earliest and most burdensome of the exploitative monopolies or "*banalités*"—the peasants' obligation to grind their corn at the lord's mill. Many peasants, however, probably still owned primitive hand mills on their own holdings. It was the lords' search for ways to increase the size of the surplus they could extract from the peasant economy that produced a *general* economic development. Bloch explains:

> The establishment of this monopoly coincided with a technological advance, the final substitution of hydraulic power for human or animal effort as the driving force. The complicated machinery of the water-mill would obviously only be worth installing if it was to be used by a large group of people, and the river or stream which drove it was often regarded as part of the lord's demesne property. But it was the element of compulsion rather than the technical advance that was really decisive: without compulsion, who knows how long the peasants might not have clung to their domestic mills?[54]

Indeed, the hand mill became a symbol of peasant resistance to feudal exploitation:

> The Benedictine Abbot of St Albans near London had himself chosen to symbolize a victory over his tenants by confiscating their hand-mills and using them to pave his parlour floor. By another symbolic act, the tenants, during the great rebellion of 1381, invaded the monastery and tore up the paving of their ancestors' hand-mills.[55]

The lords' greatest contribution to feudal economic development was their participation in the vast movement of land reclamation and occupation witnessed in medieval Europe between the years 1000 and 1250.[56] Again, their control over superior productive resources permitted the recovery of considerable terrains on the margins of the technical capacities of medieval producers—for example, the draining of wetlands, such as marshes and fens. "Reclamation and conversion of uncultivated soil," writes Perry Anderson, "were . . . the most fruitful single avenue of expansion of the rural economy in the Middle Ages, and the most dramatic expression of the improved productive capacity of feudal agriculture."[57] To the extent that the landlords employed surplus to develop the society's productive forces, however, their investments were typically "in width," that is, they expanded the stock of existing resources, rather than "in depth," investments designed to promote technical innovation. And the greatest productive uses of surplus made were as a rule connected with land reclamations.[58] The reasons for this pattern of investment, characteristic of the feudal regime, are not difficult to discern: Given the feudal nexus of sovereignty and property, "the struggle for power and the struggle for land are, of course, intertwined."[59] Landlordship, as we have seen, manifested itself "as power and wealth by virtue of the loyalty and toil which men contributed in return for land."[60] As a fief, land rewarded loyal supporters; as a manor, it meant extra revenues from new or enlarged holdings.

In all countries of Europe, feudal production is characterised by division of the soil amongst the greatest possible number of subfeudatories. The might of the feudal lord, like that of the sovereign, depended not on the length of his rent-roll, but on the number of his subjects, and the latter depended on the number of peasant proprietors.[61]

Unlike the introduction of the water mill, however, the reclamation movement did not necessarily achieve economic progress by penalizing the peasantry. Active peasant resistance often obliged the lords to maximize rent by using the carrot, not the stick. The essential requisite of colonization was a ready supply of colonizers, who were not always so readily forthcoming. Lords were therefore induced to offer peasants land "on favourable terms of tenure (mainly free status), on low fixed money rents and with no labour services, together with a degree of local autonomy."[62]

These, then, were the nobility's main contributions to feudal economic growth. Does it follow that the development of the productive forces explains feudal class relations, in the sense that these specific relations prevailed because they facilitated optimal material progress at the time? The evidence recommends against this conclusion. The lords ruled because their superior military power enabled them to appropriate a sizeable share of the social product. But the conditions of rule of the lords corresponded quite poorly to the needs of the economy. On the one hand, the nobility had only a limited economic role in feudal society. The lords as a class were outside the processes of material reproduction. They had a virtual monopoly of political and military power, but feudal agriculture was for all practical purposes independently administered by the peasant village communities. Even the demesne depended, on the whole, on the productive resources directly transferred to it from the peasant holdings; its maintenance was normally reduced to the rhythm of production of the village.[63] The nobility could therefore make only marginal contributions to productive development. On the other hand, we shall see that the lords employed the economic surplus extracted from the peasants in decidedly unproductive ways, inhibiting the adoption of available technologies and retarding the development of new ones. It cannot then be argued that feudal lords comprised the class "best suited . . . to preside over the development of the productive forces. . . . "[64] The aristocracy did, of course, preside over medieval economic growth, but it was not, or not principally, directly or indirectly responsible for it.

In fact, Marx located the main impetus of medieval economic expansion within the subordinate class of immediate producers.[65] The principal innovations in the feudal forces of production were introduced by and in turn reinforced the collective practices of the peasant villages: the iron plow or *carruca* and the improved harnessing techniques necessary to draw it, which made possible the reclamation of heavy soils, the clayey terrains of medieval Europe; the larger fields appropriate to the new ploughing techniques; the two- and three-field system of crop rotation; cropping changes such as the substitution of wheat for rye as the primary winter crop—these innovations created a new set of productive forces which permitted a striking increase in agricultural productivity.[66]

What, then, was the essential feature of the peasants' conditions of existence that made it both possible and induced them to contribute in this manner to productive development? The peasants managed their own economic life, providing for their own livelihood with means of labor they possessed and worked on their own account. Within the harsh constraints of the manorial regime, they were thus afforded an incentive to increase the surplus at their disposal by raising the productivity of the domestic economy. Peasant class struggle was the practical expression of the cultivators' attempt to devote as much as possible of their families' labor and its product to the reproduction of the holding. The forms of peasant resistance varied widely, from appeals to customary usage in the manorial or public courts, to collective noncompliance with the lords' demands, to outright rebellion.[67] Their success would determine the amount of surplus retained within the village economy, and thus, writes Marx, "to what extent the direct producer shall be enabled to improve his own condition."[68] Accordingly, feudalism's productive potential improved to the extent that the peasantry tilted the balance of class relations in their favor, wresting from the lords a greater power to determine the allocation of society's productive resources. Marx explains:

> Take it, for instance, that the enforced labour for the landlord originally amounted to two days per week. These two days of enforced labour per week are therby fixed. . . . But the productivity of the remaining days of the week, which are at the disposal of the direct producer himself, is a variable magnitude, which must develop in the course of his experience. . . . The possibility is here presented for definite economic development taking place.[69]

A general trend of medieval history contributing to economic progress was the evolution of the manorial economy from direct demesne cultivation to rent. Greater control over the production process encouraged peasants to increase their output. Marx observes that, in contrast to labor rent, "rent in kind presupposes a higher stage of civilisation for the direct producer, i.e., a higher level of development of his labour and of society in general."[70] The labor time devoted by the cultivator to his holding, and his unpaid labor for the lord, always poorly performed, "are no longer palpably separated by time and space": the peasant produces the whole of the surplus, which is divided into his and the lord's portion "on his own responsibility." In this situation, "the direct producer more or less disposes of his entire labour-time." He is thus enabled to introduce a greater element of economic rationality into the organization of his productive activity, freed from "the burdensome, . . . more or less disturbing interruption by work for the landlord." In sum, "compared with labour rent, the producer . . . has more room for action to gain time for surplus-labor whose product shall belong to himself."[71]

The dominating influence of tradition and custom over medieval life could also, under a given balance of class relations, promote economic development.[72] Seigneurial levies tended to acquire a certain stability and regularity over time, whose customary character was typically altered only by radical shifts in the relative strength of the contending classes. "It is furthermore clear that here as always it is in the interest of the ruling section of society to sanction the existing order as law and to legally establish its limits given through usage and tradition."[73] Rents were therefore fixed over long periods of time, creating a margin for the peasantry to add to the surplus retained by them by increasing the productivity of the holding.

Still, the peasantry's contribution to productive development should not be overemphasized. To begin with, little surplus was left in the peasants' hands after the lords' exactions. Only the wealthier strata of the village communities, always a minority, could afford significant outlays. Secondly, peasant investment, like the lords', tended to be extensive rather than intensive, primarily devoted to the acquisition of new land. The material basis of the peasant family, as we have seen, was the holding. Its principal economic interest, therefore, was to devote all of its resources to the reproduction of the holding as a viable economic unit. The most common strategy peasants adopted to secure this goal was to increase the self-sufficiency of the household by providing for the whole of the family's subsistence on their own account. Accordingly, peasant property both discouraged the development of the social division of labor and dictated a preference for investing in additional land rather than making progressive improvements on it, thus fettering economic dynamism.[74]

CONTRADICTION AND CRISIS

A contradiction in a mode of production manifests itself when the imperatives of surplus appropriation and the requirements of economic development become mutually incompatible and cannot be reconciled. For the ways in which individuals use their material resources to improve their circumstances then deviate dangerously from the use of resources necessary to improve society's productive power. The resulting impasse, in which the productive forces stall and contract, precipitates a crisis paralyzing the mode of production as a whole.

The fundamental contradiction of the feudal system of exploitation is that the lords were required to appropriate an economic surplus by means which restricted and eventually crippled the peasantry's capacity to reproduce the society's material base. Specifically, the lords were obliged to maintain or increase rents by extracting from the village economy more surplus than they returned to it the form of productive investments. What was rational for the lords, given their needs and capacities to preserve their position as rulers, was ultimately irrational for feudal society as a whole.

This contradiction was grounded in the cleavage between the nobility's monopoly over military and political power and the peasantry's primary responsibility for renewing society's material life.[75] This is, of course, the same division that permitted the direct producers to make a progressive contribution to economic growth. There is nothing mysterious here: it confirms the Marxian thesis that a society's class relations determine its law of development. Feudal class struggle provided both the prime mover of the medieval economy and specified the barrier point of its ultimate capacities. Beyond this limit, feudal class relations clashed with the productive forces, administering progressively severe shocks to both economy and society.

The extraeconomic mechanisms the lords depended upon to appropriate a surplus meant that it was not only practicable but necessary for them to maximize their income by siphoning from the village economy more wealth than they restored to it. It was practicable because the coercive apparatus at their disposal empowered them to apply the requisite pressure. Indeed, their exclusion from the process of production severely impaired their capacity to make a progressive economic contribution. The lords' minimal entrepreneurial function in the economy of the manor meant that they could not readily augment their revenues by increasing its productivity. Rather, they were required to use the wealth at their disposal to maintain the military-political-juridical complex that was the foundation of their class power.

The impact of seigneurial levies on the village economy was primarily disruptive.[76] As Marx noted, feudal rents had to be treated as an obligatory prior expense that wholly determined the share of the surplus retained by the peasant holdings.[77] Rents were inescapable and sometimes arbitrary; they could not be adjusted to suit the tenants' changing needs and capacities. The peasants therefore had little flexibility to respond to shifting economic circumstances. "The tenant's need of food and fodder," explains Postan, "had to be covered by what was left after the obligatory charges had been met."[78] Moreover, the lords' power to restrict the peasants' personal mobility, the free disposition of their land and goods, and to control inheritance, impaired the cultivators' capacity to deploy their resources in a rational manner, for example, to exploit available market opportunities or to consolidate holdings. Lastly, the lords enjoyed superior rights over pastures and their demesnes were usually provided with the better lands, thus leaving the peasants to cultivate the least productive soils. The overall effect of the feudal mode of exploitation—the prior nature of seigneurial levies, the barriers to the mobility of producers and land, the maldistribution of land and livestock— was to severely cripple the peasantry's ability to maintain the society's productive forces.

The village economy could support the dominant classes and institutions only by producing more than was necessary for its own reproduction. The lords' very distance from the process of production, however, only contributed to their negative economic impact by affording them little means or incentive to gauge the destructive effects of their levies on the peasant holdings.[79] Absolute increases in rent not only depressed the peasantry's economic conditions, but also, given their exclusive role in providing the society's labor power and means of production, threatened the funds necessary to refurbish feudalism's material base. Feudal rent, wrote Marx, "may assume dimensions which seriously imperil reproduction of the conditions of labour, the means of production themselves, rendering the expansion of production more or less impossible and reducing the direct producers to the physical minimum of means of subsistence."[80] Postan has estimated that the average proportion of the gross output of the typical peasant's holding levied by seigneurial exactions in England "was frequently near or above the 50 percent mark."[81]

The lords used the surplus wrested from the village to improve the extraeconomic power which buttressed their position as lords. As a result, they diverted increasing amounts of surplus away from the economy to nonproductive ends:[82] First, there were military expenditures. War was the social vocation of the medieval ruling class: military power was both the foundation of the coercive apparatus they brought to bear on the peasantry, and the typical medium of intraclass rivalry. Compared with the customary character of seigneurial levies, whose stability over time could only be altered by decisive shifts in the relative strength of the contending classes, territorial conquests afforded sudden and massive new yields to successful lords, both in terms of the new followers they could secure by providing fiefs for warriors, and the added wealth extracted from the new peasant villages they could exploit. War, writes Anderson, "was possibly the most rational and rapid single mode of expansion of surplus extraction available for any given ruling class under feudalism."[83] Yet there were few or no productive spin-offs from the building of new castles or the invention of new techniques or implements of warfare.

Second, there were outlays on display and largess. The lord's magnificence was instrumental in his capacity to recruit and mobilize retinues, for his liberality in gifts and expenditures provided an indispensable part of his followers' livelihood; or to conclude marriages by providing daughters with attractive dowries, thereby forming or cementing family alliances. Yet the lords' largess not only deprived agriculture of needed resources; their demand for luxury articles also meant that urban production made few progressive contributions to the rural economy. Clearly, specialized production of highly crafted goods did not provide the kind of means of production required to increase the productivity of peasant holdings. Moreover, the lords' rising demand would tend to divert an increasing proportion of rural food producers to the cities without significantly increasing the countryside's capacity to support them; the florescence of medieval urban industry was thus built on a progressively narrower economic base.

Third, there were administrative expenditures, which included not only the expense of maintaining an increasingly complex superstructure of church and state, but of tightening the management of the manor. The latter, the most important innovation of which was the introduction of accounts, was a more purely economic investment, but its contribution was largely confined to rationalizing the exploitation of the manorial economy, not to raising its productivity.

Lastly, there were outlays for religious ends, which included not only the building of cathedrals and churches, but land endowments to religious orders and monasteries. The Church occupied a pivotal position in medieval society. It owned a large share of the land in every European country, and its higher clergy was tightly interwoven into the fabric of aristocratic life. As landowners, bishops and abbots also exercised extensive rights of jurisdiction over a dependent peasant population. The religious sincerity of the aristocracy, or its fervent desire for the salvation the Church offered, should not, of course, be trivialized. But as a constituent fraction of the ruling class, the Church played not only a secular role as landlord, but also a powerful ideological role in legitimating the existing distribution of social and political obligations.

The preceding catalogue of landlord outlays is not meant to be exhaustive; nor are the types of expenditures listed according to scale of magnitude. The lords directed their wealth to one or another purpose according to individual preferences, circumstances, and the existing balance of class forces. Rather, this list purports to show the sorts of outlays that absorbed the lion's share of estate revenues. Its significance lies in highlighting the feature that is their hallmark: none provided "any significant feedback in the form of investment which would increase production."[84]

We have seen that the peasantry, for its part, sustained the main impulse of feudal economic expansion. Given the lords' monopoly of military and political power and the peasants' direct control of the production process, and given the customary character of seigneurial levies, the most practicable avenue open to the direct producers to increase their share of the social product was to increase the productivity of the village economy. The "profit" of the peasant holding, so to speak, "grew up behind the back of rent."[85] Nevertheless, as Marx emphasized, peasant production imposed its own limits on economic development:

> This mode of production pre-supposes parcelling of the soil, and scattering of the other means of production. As it excludes the concentration of these means of production, so also it excludes co-operation, division of labour within each separate process of production, the control over, and the productive application of the forces of Nature by society, and the free development of the social productive powers. It is compatible only with a system of production, and a society, moving within narrow and more or less primitive bounds.[86]

To begin with, the small scale of peasant property and the common field system of cultivation permitted only modest technical progress. The more ambitious innovations associated with the agricultural revolution, we shall see, presupposed both compact farms and capital outlays beyond the means of the average cultivator.[87]

Second, the outlays of the peasant family were as a rule designed to increase the self-sufficiency of the holding. The economic foundation of the peasant family lay in its capacity to reproduce its own means of subsistence and production. One of the hallmarks of the peasant outlook, we have seen, "was a deeply rooted sense of family property rights in the . . . holding, and the various appurtenances which made it a viable economic unit."[88] This outlook was reinforced by the low level of agricultural productivity, which made harvests, and therefore food surpluses, highly uncertain. Peasants thus tended to avoid dependence on external sources of subsistence, especially on the market. They associated the development of the productive forces at their disposal with the goal of preserving the independence of the family holding. Self-sufficiency, however, dictated a preference for nonspecialized production within the confines of a domestic economy, thereby limiting the development of the social division of labor. Entrenched in their holdings, peasants tended to preserve the fragmentation of the society's productive resources. Moreover, to the extent that peasant families sought to curtail their recourse to existing markets, they restricted the mobility of labor and land, thereby inhibiting the economy's flexibility to respond to changing circumstances. Indeed, typically, only resources above the reproductive needs of the holding were exchanged on the market, and to the extent that technical means—for example, transport—made exchange possible, peasant mobility and transactions were normally confined to the immediate locality.[89]

Lastly, the peasants used a major part of their resources to acquire additional land. This form of investment was intimately associated with their deep sense of ownership in the family holding. The material well-being of the peasant family was in most cases reducible to land. The major economic demand among peasants was for a plot, if they possessed none, and a larger plot if they did. The pressure generated by this demand created a veritable land hunger, particularly when medieval population growth reached its zenith towards the end of the thirteenth century. To be sure, the demand for land led to the reclamation of uncultivated terrains, propelling the main thrust of feudal expansion. At the same time, however, the peasantry diverted increasing amounts of productive resources towards the purchase or lease of increasingly more expensive land, and thus subtracted from the funds available for making progressive improvements on it.[90] In sum, small peasant production, Marx wrote, contained an inherent tendency towards "gradual impoverishment and exhaustion of the soil subjected to this cultivation."[91]

The impact of the lords' exactions on the limited economic potential of peasant property determined the limits of feudal development. What was necessary to reproduce the society's productive forces became impossible, given the needs and capacities of its contending classes to appropriate the maximum surplus; they could not, so to speak, restore to the economy what they pumped out of it. The result was a massive crisis which convulsed European society in the fourteenth century. Sometime during its early decades the basic motor of land reclamation that had powered the feudal economy for three centuries faltered and finally stalled. The forces of production thereafter entered upon a prolonged period of regression, taking the form of a quickening movement of decolonization, as village after village was completely evacuated.

The contraction of the area under plough was the price of its very success. Medieval agriculture presupposed a symbiosis between arable farming and pasture: grass maintained the animals necessary not only as a direct source of food and energy, but primarily for fertilizer; dung was the main soil additive. Yet the simultaneous pressure of the lords' exactions and the peasants' demand for land both impaired the villagers' capacity to invest in animals and led to the extension of arable cultivation into lands formerly reserved for pasture. The result was an ecological imbalance that precipitated a general deterioration of the soil. Postan explains:

> So inherent was the shifting frontier between grass and grain in the very process of medieval growth and reclamation that most readers will be prepared to take it for granted. What is less self-evident is that in the course of the thirteenth century and perhaps even earlier the frontier not only approached but in many places crossed its limits of safety, and that by the end of that and the beginning of the following

century, in corn–growing parts of the country taken as a whole, pasture and the animal population had been reduced to a level incompatible with the conduct of mixed farming itself.[92]

Declining agricultural yields were unable to support the existing population. The ecological imbalance precipitated a demographic collapse: population growth, built on an increasingly precarious economic base, tipped over into overpopulation. Poor harvests resulted in famine, pushing the death rate to punishing heights. The depopulation of the countryside was given a frightening impetus by the Black Death that swept Europe between 1348 and 1350. Its initial devastation, approximately one-third of the population, was followed by a series of aftershocks—repeated outbreaks of pestilence whose combined toll by 1400 was perhaps two-fifths.[93]

The crisis unleashed a desperate rent struggle as the contending classes sought to protect their economic conditions in the face of a receding productive base. The main circumstance underlying their clash was the dramatic shortfall in the availability of labor caused by the demographic collapse. The most rational avenue open to the lords to defend their position in the face of a rapidly rising land-to-labor ratio, given their monopoly of political and military power, was to fasten the peasantry to the manor and enforce wage reductions, and to recoup the deficiencies of agricultural income by reaping the profits of war—ransom, booty, offices, and fiefs of defeated rivals. The English Statutes of Labourers of 1349–1351 and the French Ordonnance of 1351 contained a main provision aimed at battering down wages and reinforcing clauses which sought to prevent the mobility of labor. They were, writes Anderson, "among the most glacially explicit programmes of exploitation in the whole history of European class struggle."[94] And the Hundred Years War, from the military and political as well as economic perspective, the "biggest and best" of medieval conflicts, released a free-floating lumpen nobility, demobilized warriors who abandoned both liege lord and manor to make their fortune by banditry.

The peasants, for their part, resisted the seigneurial offensive by using their new economic leverage, the scarcity of labor, to obtain additional land and lax conditions of tenure. Their struggle was organized village by village, built upon the long years of experience of conflict with the lords, and punctuated by mass movements of regional or national scope. The Grande Jacquerie, which convulsed Northern France in 1358, and the English Peasants Revolt of 1381 "were only the major episodes of a continent-wide phenomenon which stretched from Denmark to Majorca."[95]

All the major peasant insurrections were swiftly and brutally suppressed. Nevertheless, throughout Western Europe, the peasantry succeeded in loosening the grip of aristocratic domination.[96] The direct producers were thus able to achieve substantial progress in their material conditions of life. Not only were the lords, once defeated, compelled to grant considerable concessions to attract settlers, but the peasantry aggressively enforced improvements in their economic conditions. The result was the beginning of a "golden age" for West European peasants: they acquired both larger plots of land and greater freedom to dispose of their labor and its product.[97]

Why, then, did the Western peasantry triumph? Cohen suggests that one of the main challenges confronting the thesis that class struggle governs historical change is "to explain, other than by reference to the disposition of classes to develop the productive forces, what makes successful classes succeed."[98] Two alternative explanations of the conclusion of feudal class struggle are current among Marxist historians. The first assigns primary responsibility to the impact of an independent urban sector upon the contending classes.[99] Towns decisively altered the matrix of class forces on the land by offering a permanent possibility of flight for disaffected peasants. The presence of urban centers therefore specified the objective limits of the lords' power: anxious to maintain tenants for the rents they provided, the lords were forced to relax seigneurial levies upon the peasantry.

This thesis is difficult to accept in full.[100] First, the modest demographic weight of the towns was insufficient to exert the sort of gravitational pull which could account for the general dissolution of the seigneurial ties binding the peasantry to the manor. Second, the towns offered few economic opportunities for peasant refugees. The urban economy was primarily organized toward the production of a limited number of luxury goods. The workmanship required to produce highly crafted articles provided the rationale for the guilds and the complex rules of apprenticeship whereby they regulated and severely restricted the possibilities of employment. Indeed, as we have seen, rural mobility, even after the peasantry's success in loosening the lords' jurisdictional power, was largely confined to the countryside, sometimes from one holding to another in the same village.[101] Third, the urban patriciates would either align themselves with the aristocracy against the peasantry or, at best, make use of the great insurrections to press their own ends. Lastly, even the record of support by the urban poor for peasant rebels was not impressive.[102]

The second interpretation, more in keeping with Marx's theory of class struggle, underscores the differences in the relative organizational capacities of the contending classes.[103] Western Europe was densely populated by an "old" peasantry. The collective life of peasants was deeply rooted: they "had had many centuries to evolve institutions, common practices and a consciousness of their own interests."[104] Moreover, not only were peasant villages older than the ruling aristocracy; given the tendency of noble families to die out or to be replaced by conquest, peasant communities had a more continuous life and were more deeply entrenched. The West European peasantry thus developed the requisite solidarity and strength to successfully resist seigneurial encroachments. In sum, this interpretation ascribes primary responsibility for the peasants' triumph to the social relations they established in working and protecting their lands; not to the great peasant rebellions—"flashes in the pan," Bloch called them—but to "the patient, silent struggles stubbornly carried on by rural communities over the years."[105]

THE LIMITATIONS OF PEASANT CLASS STRUGGLE

The resolution of the feudal class struggle in Western Europe, that is, the triumph of the peasantry, raises the question whether and in what sense it created the real possibility for a qualitative social transformation. The great crash of European feudalism did not release any vigorous development of society's forces of production. The crisis complex, Anderson correctly observed, did not comprise the expansion of a new ensemble of productive forces colliding against and bursting through an obsolete set of class relations. Rather, feudal class relations determined both the possibilities and limits of growth; the great crash took the form of a cataclysmic *destruction* of the productive forces. New forces of production would emerge only *after* class relations were radically altered, that is, after the formation of a new class system engendered a new configuration of labor power and means of production in agriculture and industry.[106]

Marx's theory of class, then, correctly specified the law of motion of the feudal mode of production, the internal dynamic that impelled its growth and precipitated its decline. However, given that Marx elaborated this theory as an integral part of his attempt to explain radical historical change, the question it raises is: Did feudal class struggle nurture within itself a class with the potential to revolutionize society as a whole? Did the peasantry, in other words, provide the basis for the historical leap towards a wholly new economy and society? It obviously did not. The most authoritative historian of medieval peasant movements, R. H. Hilton, concluded in his study of peasant class struggles thus:

> It may seem a platitude to say that the only social force emerging from the medieval world which was capable of taking over from the aristocracy was the bourgeoisie; this was not only what did happen, but any examination of the peasantry as an alternative ruling group must show that this was the only development that could happen.[107]

To be sure, the extreme localism of peasant movements, typical of a class organized around family units of production in village communities, impaired their capacity to achieve a profound reordering of class relations. Nevertheless, the peasantry could not constitute itself "as an alternative ruling group" for a more fundamental reason. The nature of the feudal class relationship is such that the contending classes are defined and defined themselves in terms of their immediate opposition of interests *within* the mode of production itself. The direct producers experienced and measured their exploitation in terms of the lords' claims on their labor power and its product. The very presence of the exploiting class provided the main impetus animating village solidarity. The inherent tensions within peasant communities, especially between wealthy and poor, were checked by the collective requirement to resist the nobility. Indeed, whatever their internal divisions, they shared common conditions of existence as against the lords. This meant, however, that the peasantry's interests as a class were circumscribed by the need to loosen or break the grip of aristocratic domination. Their struggle did *not*, in other words, encompass a need or project to create a wholly new social formation.

The principal strains of the peasants' outlook reflected this situation. Peasant class consciousness was primarily "a negative class consciousness in that the definition of class which was involved was that of their enemies rather than of themselves."[108] Its distinguishing hallmark was a bitter hatred of the landowning nobility; but the peasantry did not have any clear *positive* view that their situation could be qualitatively different than it was.[109] The precipitating causes of peasant movements were typically actions by members of the ruling class "which altered the customary relationships or disappointed normal expectations, to the detriment of the peasant class as a whole, rich and poor."[110] Peasants perceived alterations in the social fabric from a conservative standpoint: "they cannot accept the abandonment of traditional roles by any one of the orders of the society—whose basic structure they do not . . . challenge."[111] Their chief aims were as a rule confined to removing particular individuals from power, especially those closely associated with the judicial process, and destroying the manorial court rolls where their obligations were recorded. Jurisdictional authority was, as we have seen, the basis of the lords' power to command the peasants' labor. Most peasant class activity in effect took the form of "individual village movements aimed at altering the balance of the relationships between the peasant community and the individual lord, rather than transforming or abolishing these relationships."[112] To the extent that peasant movements acquired a wider, regional or national scope, their prime motivating ideology was religion. Yet the ruling religious ideas of medieval cultivators tended to be "the ideas of the rulers of society as transmitted to them in innumerable sermons about the duties and characteristic sins of the various orders of society."[113] Insofar as religious beliefs were used to challenge the existing legitimating tradition, the ideological weapons of the ruling class were used against it by turning the symbolism of the church upside down. Medieval crusades and heretical movements often attracted large numbers of the peasant poor; they drew their inspiration from the example of Jesus of Nazareth, "a redeemer who in life had had no property, whose followers had been equally poor, and who could best be approached by those with no or few worldly goods."[114] Above all, then, the peasants could not be said to have a realizable notion of what could replace the regime they were attacking.[115] Existing resentments of a diffuse nature were focused and translated into common action by moves on the lords' part to tighten seigneurial exactions, not by the practical experience of an alternative order which could be brought into being.

This is one of the most significant conclusions yielded by a study of the feudal crisis in Western Europe: There is no intrinsic dynamic impelling the type of class struggle grounded in the relationship of surplus extraction toward social revolution. There is, therefore, no reason to anticipate that the class of direct producers will develop the capacity and interest to undertake a struggle to construct a wholly new society as the culmination of their struggle against their conditions of exploitation. The best evidence for this argument is that, once the lords were decisively defeated, the peasant class disintegrated from within. That is, once the rationale for their solidarity as a class disappeared, the internal divisions within the peasants progressively manifested themselves, prying apart the village communities. Indeed, it was often wealthier cultivators who took the lead in the enclosures that initiated the dissolution of the peasantry. The triumph of the peasants as a class was thus their last act as a cohesive historical force. It was, ironically, only by losing its capacity for concerted, sustained struggle that the peasantry created the circumstances necessary for the transition to capitalism.[116]

If, then, the class struggle between feudalism's appropriating and producing classes did not impel its qualitative transformation, we are still left with the question of the nature of the class struggle which gave rise to the bourgeoisie and empowered it to take over from the aristocracy. It is to this issue that we now turn.

NOTES

1. Marc Bloch, *French Rural History*, p. 170.
2. This is White, *Medieval Technology and Social Change*.
3. G. A. Cohen, *Karl Marx's Theory of History*, p. 167, n. 2.
4. Ibid., pp. 170–171.
5. Ibid., p. 171. See also G. A. Cohen, "Reply to Four Critics," p. 199.
6. Ibid., pp. 148–149.
7. Postan, *The Medieval Economy and Society*, p. 42.
8. M. M. Postan and John Hatcher, "Population and Class Relations in Feudal Society," in *The Brenner Debate*, ed. Aston and Philpin, p. 65. See also Postan, *The Medieval Economy and Society*, p. 27. Perhaps the most influential representative of this view in France is Emmanuel Le Roy Ladurie. See, for example, *The Peasants of Languedoc*.
9. The rival claims of Marxian and demographic explanations of the feudal dynamic were forcefully debated in a symposium in *Past and Present*, occasioned by Robert Brenner's article, "Agrarian Class Structure and Economic Development in Pre-Industrial Europe." The symposium articles are now collected in *The Brenner Debate* ed. Aston and Philpin. A second, older tradition of historians maintained that feudalism possessed no inherent dynamic that made for its evolution and decline. Rather, long-term economic fluctuations and shifts in the balance of class relations were explained in terms of "exogenous" factors, specifically by changes in the level and pace of seaborne commerce. I leave this thesis without further comment for now. The question of the role of commerce in the supersession of feudalism by capitalism will be taken up below, in Chapter 4.
10. See Postan and Hatcher, pp. 69–70, 73, 77–78. See also Postan, *The Medieval Economy and Society*, pp. 41–44.
11. See Postan, *The Medieval Economy and Society*, pp. 99–109, 138–142, 148–154; see also Le Roy Ladurie, *The Peasants of Languedoc*, pp. 36–40, 74ff., 132, 289.
12. Much of the best discussion of these processes is to be found in Postan, *The Medieval Economy and Society*, pp. 57–72.

13. Brenner, "The Agrarian Roots of European Capitalism", in *The Brenner Debate*, pp. 217–24.

14. Postan and Hatcher, p. 78; Postan, *The Medieval Economy and Society*, pp. 103, 135; Le Roy Ladurie, *The Peasants of Languedoc*, pp. 296–309.

15. Postan and Hatcher accuse Brenner of a "morbid" focus on class analysis to explain medieval economic trends (p. 73). It is unclear to me, however, why this approach is any more morbid than one which focuses on the ratio of deaths to births.

16. Postan and Hatcher, p. 78.

17. See below, The Feudal Dynamic.

18. Marx, Vol. 1 of *Capital* p. 592. See also Marx, *Grundrisse*, p. 605.

19. Brenner, "The Agrarian Roots of European Capitalism," pp. 224–26.

20. Marx, *Capital* 1:316, n. 3, and 699–700. See also Marx, *Capital* 3:786–87, and Anderson, *Passages From Antiquity to Feudalism*, p. 147.

21. Hilton, *Bond Men Made Free*, pp. 35–36.

22. Hilton, "A Crisis of Feudalism," p. 121; Brenner, "Agrarian Class Structure and Economic Development," pp. 38–39.

23. Brenner, "The Origins of Capitalist Development," p. 47.

24. Marx, *Capital* 3:785–86. See also, Brenner, "The Origins of Capitalist Development," pp. 60, 70.

25. Marx, *Capital* 1:697–701. See also Marx, *Grundrisse*, p. 479; Marrington, "Town and Country in the Transition to Capitalism," in *The Transition From Feudalism to Capitalism*, ed. Hilton, pp. 171–72.

26. Marx, *Capital* 3:795.

27. Postan, *The Medieval Economy and Society*, p. 129.

28. Marc Bloch, "The Rise of Dependent Cultivation and Seigniorial Institutions," in *The Agrarian Life of the Middle Ages*, Vol. 1 of *The Cambridge Economic History of Europe*, ed. J. H. Clapham and Eileen Power (Cambridge: Cambridge University Press, 1944), p. 224.

29. Anderson, *Passages*, p. 183.

30. Postan, *The Medieval Economy and Society*, pp. 144–45, cf., Bloch, *French Rural History*, pp. 70–71.

31. Marx, *Capital* 3:795.

32. Rodney Hilton, *The Decline of Serfdom in Medieval England*, p. 10.

33. Joan Thirsk, "The Common Fields," pp. 10–11.

34. Hilton, *Bond Men Made Free*, p. 31; Bloch, *French Rural History*, pp. 45–48.

35. Postan offers a detailed account of the impact of the technical infrastructure on the organization of production in the peasant village. See *The Medieval Economy and Society*, pp. 44–57.

36. Hilton, *Bond Men Made Free*, p. 34.
37. Ibid., p. 61; Bloch, *French Rural History*, p. 169.
38. Marx characterizes the feudal regime thus as early as 1843, in "On the Jewish Question," Vol. 3 of Marx and Engels, *Collected Works*, pp. 165–66. (Hereafter *CW*.) See also Marx, *Economic and Philosophic Manuscripts* of 1844, *CW* 3:266–67. A good account of the process of formation of the lordship is found in Anderson, *Passages*, pp. 139–42. See also Bloch, "The Rise of Dependent Cultivation and Seigniorial Institutions," *passim*.
39. This is F. W. Maitland's formulation, quoted by Postan, *The Medieval Economy and Society*, p. 79.
40. Anderson, *Lineages of the Absolutist State*, p. 408.
41. Marx, *The German Ideology*, *CW* 5:34.
42. Marx, *Capital* 3:790.
43. Postan, *The Medieval Economy and Society*, p. 89.
44. Marx, *Capital* 3:790.
45. Ibid., p. 791.
46. Ibid., p. 790.
47. Ibid., p. 791. Cf., Hilton, "A Crisis of Feudalism," pp. 124–25.
48. Hilton, *Bond Men Made Free*, p. 60.
49. Ibid., pp. 38, 40.
50. Ibid., p. 70.
51. Postan, *The Medieval Economy and Society*, pp. 95, 124.
52. Hilton, introduction to *The Transition From Feudalism to Capitalism*, pp. 16–17. See also Hilton, *Bond Men Made Free*, pp. 48–49.
53. See Fernand Braudel, *The Structures of Everyday Life*, pp. 353–61.
54. Bloch, *French Rural History*, pp. 79–80.
55. Hilton, "Feudalism in Europe: Problems for Historical Materialists," p. 88.
56. Bloch, *French Rural History*, pp. 5–17; Postan, *The Medieval Economy and Society*, pp. 18–25.
57. Anderson, *Passages*, p. 188.
58. Postan, *The Medieval Economy and Society*, p. 103; see also, pp. 43–44.
59. Hilton, "A Comment," in *The Transition From Feudalism to Capitalism*, p. 114.
60. Hilton, *Bond Men Made Free*, p. 45.
61. Marx, *Capital* 1:671–72.
62. Hilton, *Bond Men Made Free*, pp. 43–44.
63. Hilton, "A Crisis of Feudalism," pp. 126–27.

64. G. A. Cohen, *Karl Marx's Theory of History*, p. 149.
65. Marx, *Capital* 3:793–96, 798–99, 806–07.
66. Postan, *The Medieval Economy and Society*, pp. 44–52.
67. See Hilton, *A Medieval Society*, pp. 154–60.
68. Marx, *Capital* 3:793; see also, p. 790.
69. Ibid., p. 794.
70. Ibid.
71. Ibid., p. 795.
72. Ibid., p. 793. See also Bloch, *French Rural History*, pp. 70–71.
73. Marx, *Capital* 3:793. Marx emphasizes, of course, that a mode of production is always necessarily a system of reproduction: "Apart from all else, this, by the way, comes about of itself as soon as the constant reproduction of the basis of the existing order and its fundamental relations assumes a regulated and orderly form in the course of time." Ibid.
74. See the following: Marx, *Capital* 3:796; Brenner, "The Origins of Capitalist Development," p. 36; Postan, *The Medieval Economy and Society*, p. 135; Hilton, *Bond Men Made Free*, pp. 34–35.
75. See Hilton, "A Crisis of Feudalism," in *The Brenner Debate*, ed. Aston and Philpin, pp. 125–27; Brenner, "The Agrarian Roots of European Capitalism," in *The Brenner Debate*, ed. Aston and Philpin, pp. 232–42.
76. Marx, *Capital* 3:795; cf. Marx, *Capital* 1:226ff.
77. Marx, *Capital* 3:790.
78. Postan, *The Medieval Economy and Society*, p. 126.
79. Brenner, "The Origins of Capitalist Development," pp. 46–47.
80. Marx, *Capital* 3:796. Cf. Marx, *Capital* 1:229, 253.
81. Postan, *The Medieval Economy and Society*, p. 125. Postan is referring to England, where a well organized ruling class faced a defensive peasantry. In France, by contrast, strong, aggressive peasant communities facing a relatively disorganized ruling class succeeded in retaining a considerably greater portion of their output. Consequently, the French economy was both more productive and able to sustain a much larger population than the English. See Brenner, "The Agrarian Roots of European Capitalism," in *The Brenner Debate*, ed. Aston and Philpin, pp. 242–54, 264–66.
82. The following catalogue of landlord outlays is distilled from: Hilton, "A Crisis of Feudalism," in *The Brenner Debate*, ed. Aston and Philpin, pp. 130–31; Hilton, *Bond Men Made Free*, pp. 50–53; Anderson, *Lineages*, pp. 31–32; Postan, *The Medieval Economy and Society*, pp. 101–103; Postan and Hatcher, p. 78; Brenner, "The Origins of Capitalist Development," pp. 46–47.

83. Anderson, *Lineages*, p. 31.

84. Hilton, "A Crisis of Feudalism," in *The Brenner Debate*, ed. Aston and Philpin, p. 131.

85. Marx, *Capital* 3:796.

86. Marx, *Capital* 1:713–14.

87. Clarkson, *The Pre-Industrial Economy in England, 1500–1750*, pp. 59–60.

88. Hilton, *Bond Men Made Free*, p. 38.

89. Hilton, *The Decline of Serfdom*, pp. 34–35.

90. Marx, *Capital* 3:807–08, 810.

91. Ibid., p. 807.

92. Postan, *The Medieval Economy and Society*, pp. 58–59.

93. Anderson, *Passages*, p. 201. An excellent, if impressionistic, account of the Black Death's devastation and the resulting social dislocation can be found in Tuchmann, *A Distant Mirror*, ch. 5.

94. Anderson, *Passages*, pp. 201–02. See also Hilton, *Bond Men Made Free*, pp.154–55. Hilton, *The Decline of Serfdom*, pp. 35–43.

95. Anderson, *Passages*, p. 203. Much of the best discussion of these mass peasant movements in the later Middle Ages can be found in Hilton, *Bond Men Made Free*, pp. 96–134. He offers a detailed analysis of the English rebellion on pp. 137–232.

96. In contrast, Eastern Europe witnessed the triumph of the nobility over the peasantry. "This central fact," writes Anderson, "was the basic historical determinant of the uneven development of Europe, and of the persistent retardation of the East." *Passages*, p. 213. For an explanation of this particular outcome in the struggle between lords and peasants, and of its consequences for economic development, see Brenner, "Agrarian Class Structure and Economic Development," in *The Brenner Debate*, ed. Aston and Philpin, pp. 41–46, and "The Agrarian Roots of European Capitalism," in *The Brenner Debate*, ed. Aston and Philpin, pp. 275–83.

97. See: Marx, *Grundrisse*, p. 510; Anderson, *Passages*, pp. 204, 207–08; Bloch, *French Rural History*, pp. 106–07, 115–16; Hilton, *Bond Men Made Free*, pp. 153–54; Hilton, *The Decline of Serfdom*, pp. 32–35, 39; and "A Crisis of Feudalism," in *The Brenner Debate*, ed. Aston and Philpin, pp. 131–35; Postan, *The Medieval Economy and Society*, pp. 106, 138–42, 151.

98. G. A. Cohen, "Reply to Four Critics," p. 207.

99. See, for example, Anderson, *Passages*, pp. 205–06. Marx gives some support to this interpretation in *The German Ideology*, *CW* 5:34, 64–65, 79.

100. This paragraph draws primarily upon Brenner, "Agrarian Class

Structure and Economic Development," in *The Brenner Debate*, ed. Aston and Philpin, pp. 38–40, and "The Origins of Capitalist Development," pp. 47–48.

101. Hilton, *The Decline of Serfdom*, pp. 34–35.

102. Hilton, *Bond Men Made Free*, pp. 206–07.

103. See, for example: Brenner, "Agrarian Class Structure and Economic Development," pp. 40–45; Hilton, *Bond Men Made Free*, pp. 96, 109, 214–19; Hilton, "A Crisis of Feudalism," in *The Brenner Debate*, ed. Aston and Philpin, p. 132; Bloch, *French Rural History*, p. 170.

104. Hilton, *Bond Men Made Free*, p. 29.

105. Bloch, *French Rural History*, p. 170.

106. Anderson, *Passages*, pp. 203–04.

107. Hilton, *Bond Men Made Free*, p. 235.

108. Ibid., p. 130.

109. Ibid., p. 220.

110. Ibid., p. 118.

111. Ibid., p. 119.

112. Ibid., p. 96.

113. Rodney Hilton, *The English Peasantry*, p. 16.

114. Hilton, *Bond Men Made Free*, p. 97.

115. Ibid., p. 229.

116. This argument will be developed more fully below, in Chapter 5.

4

From Feudalism to Capitalism: The Role of Merchant Capital

The indispensable prerequisite of the genesis of capitalist production is a stage of primitive capital accumulation. Capital must be gathered in the hands of a capitalist class before capitalism as a mode of production can flourish.[1] Thus, the question of the transition from feudalism to capitalism can be referred back to the question of the conditions which gave rise to the accumulation of capital and facilitated it. We shall argue that Marx offered two opposing interpretations of this process. The first is developed primarily in his earlier works. It maintains that capital accumulation was encouraged by the growth of medieval towns, assigning principal responsibility for the emergence of capitalism to the mercantile bourgeoisie. The distinguishing hallmark of this analysis is that it explains changes in feudal class relations by relating them to underlying changes in society's productive forces. The argument is that advances in the social division of labor and the concomitant spread of commercial networks within the interstices of the old order gave rise to superior ways of reproducing material life. The nascent scheme of the productive forces in turn generated increasing pressure for the reorganization of the traditional regime, necessary to realize the potential for economic development fettered under its limiting conditions. The transition is thus seen as the forcible adaptation of feudal class relations to the requirements of economic progress.[2]

By contrast, Marx's later historical writings developed a second interpretation of the transition from feudalism to capitalism that inverts his widely received conception of the primacy of the forces of production. The conclusion yielded by this interpretation is that class relationships explain the development of the productive forces and not vice versa. This version contains two parts. The first consists of a series of historical investigations showing that the mercantile bourgeoisie was essentially conservative, a fraction of the feudal ruling class. In this view, the productive development that merchant capitalism facilitated did not precipitate the dissolution of the ancien regime. Quite the contrary, the continued accumulation of merchant capital and the productive forces it created depended upon the preservation of the old order, inhibiting the rise of the new. The second part of this interpretation argues that the primitive accumulation of capital presupposed a radical reordering of the feudal mode of exploitation, assigning principal responsibility for this transformation to the dynamics of class struggle in the countryside.[3]

This chapter assesses Marx's contradictory views of the role played by merchant capitalists in the transition from feudalism to capitalism. Our study intersects an ongoing debate among historians. The main dividing line in this debate corresponds to the opposing estimates of the merchants' contribution found in Marx's texts. A distinguished tradition of historical enquiry identifies the mercantile bourgeoisie as the primary agent responsible for developing the productive forces which underwrote the emergence of capitalism. Its lineages can be traced to classical political economy: According to Adam Smith and James Steuart, for example, the development of the social division of labor and the market, institutionalized in the separation of town and country, gave rise to an economic dynamism that overturned the feudal organization of society.[4] This interpretation formed an intergral part of Max Weber's understanding of the transition to capitalism: Weber maintained that the distinctive economic and political autonomy of the occidental city nurtured a capitalist nucleus which acted as a powerful solvent upon the feudal economy and society.[5] The Belgian historian, Henri Pirenne, elaborated a comprehensive theory of Western civilization which identified in the nature of its towns and the extent of their commercial networks the primary motor of its historical evolution and of the passage from feudalism to capitalism in particular.[6] Pirenne's thesis found its way into the debates within Marxism in the work of Paul Sweezy, where it formed the empirical basis for his critique of Maurice Dobb, initiating the now famous debate on the transition.[7] Finally, the equation of the division of labor and the spread of markets with the rise of capitalism is the centerpiece of the interpretation of the early modern epoch found in the works of Immanuel Wallerstein and Fernand Braudel.[8]

A rival tradition of historical interpretation locates the operations of merchant capitalists *within* the class structure of the feudal regime, denying them a revolutionary role. A. B. Hibbert and Rodney Hilton sharply criticized Pirenne's theory of the rise of trade and the nature of the changes it wrought in the economy of European feudalism.[9] Sweezy was severly taken to task by Dobb, Hilton, Kohachiro Takahashi, and others, who questioned on both theoretical and empirical grounds his tendency to ignore Marxian injunctions regarding the centrality of class relations in the explanation of economic development.[10] This is also in substance the critique Robert Brenner levelled against Wallerstein's thesis and Elizabeth Fox-Genovese and Eugene Genovese against Braudel's.[11]

This chapter is divided into four sections. The first discusses Marx's positive evaluation of merchant capital's role in adopting the productive forces that overthrew feudal society, and the second considers the historical investigations that reverse this view. The third section tests these arguments by analyzing the nature of the crisis which struck feudal Europe in the seventeenth century. The final section examines Marx's conception of the genesis of the industrial capitalist.

THE FRUITS OF MERCHANT CAPITALISM

Merchant Capitalism and the Development of the Productive Forces

The merchants' progressive contribution to the accumulation of capital was facilitated by a sociopolitical revolution in medieval Europe: the communal movement which won for the towns a separate political existence, permitting the urban economy to evolve according to its own inherent propensities.[12] The overall parcellization of sovereignties characteristic of the feudal regime made it the first mode of production in history to give urban life an independent existence within an overwhelmingly agrarian order. Towns were essentially "non-feudal islands in the feudal seas."[13] Feudal society thus gave rise to a *dynamic* opposition between urban and rural conditions of existence. The countryside comprised a natural economy dominated by land; towns, however, were first and foremost markets, largely dependent upon and organized around the production and exchange of commodities. Money played only an ancillary role in the domestic economy of lords and peasants; it was intrinsic to the commercial economy of the towns. The rural economy was centered in small, scattered villages which fragmented the society's productive forces; the towns concentrated means of production and population within their walls. The juridical structure of the countryside sharply curtailed personal mobility, the disposal of property, and freedom of contract, and rigidly divided the occupations of knight and villein; medieval towns relaxed restrictions on personal status, property, and freedom of movement and contract in order to facilitate the pursuit of trade. Agrarian life was dominated by custom; the denizens of the urban world, in contrast, developed new ways of getting rich that required innovation and risk. In sum, towns and their markets provided a prodigious stimulus to the feudal economy: greater specialization and innovation were natural by-products of the interchange between separate economic regions and centers, as producers mobilized material resources to exploit comparative economic advantages.[14]

The superior productive capacity of the urban economy ensured its ultimate victory over its rural surroundings, transferring the center of economic activity from the country to the city.[15] The growth of towns generated increasing pressure for the development of agrarian production: industry drew raw materials, manpower and its food supply from the countryside, and depended upon the rural economy to absorb its product. The manorial regime, however, was poorly suited to production for the market: agricultural techniques were primitive, the division of labor undeveloped, its administration unwieldy, and the customary rules governing land management and the labor process uneconomic. Above all, tenurial relationships inhibited the rearrangement of the factors of production to improve efficiency.

The expansion of commodity demand acted as a powerful solvent upon the economy of lords and peasants, dissolving seigneurial authority. The stultifying framework of the manor was destroyed from within by the complementary responses of enterprising lords and peasants pressing against it in order to realize the economic benefits they saw in prospect for themselves. The landlords endeavored to improve and modernize technical methods of agriculture, principally by consolidating farms and introducing specialized crops. Their success, however, presupposed greater flexibility in the use of land and labor. There was thus a general evolution in class relations away from serfdom towards contractual arrangements: commutation of labor services gave way to manumission of serfs. The peasants, for their part, advanced these developments by actively asserting their independence. The existence of autonomous towns offered them a haven from their dependent status, altering the balance of class forces on the land. The lords were compelled to make concessions to peasants with the opportunity of fleeing to the towns, concessions which typically included greater personal liberty. The emancipation of the serfs, however, simultaneously emancipated the landlords, who were now free to rationalize production on their lands. The rising tempo of economic activity promoted a process of economic differentiation within the ranks of the peasantry. The elements were thus released for the reorganization of the rural economy in terms of contractual relationships between landlords, tenant farmers, and agricultural wage laborers.

The transformation of the countryside's social physiognomy, however, was not only the result of a reorientation of lords and peasants to the pull of the market. The merchants of the towns promoted the weakening of the manor because it limited their market opportunities. The operations of merchant capital thus tended to refashion the countryside in the town's image. The land and its resources were reduced to one branch of the overall social division of labor—agriculture.

Towns, indeed, were centers of social experimentation, premonitions of a new historical order.[16] Within them emerged a new type of individual altogether—*homo economicus*. The vanguard of these centers were the merchant capitalists, enabled by long distance commerce and a system of urban relay points to develop a sense of their common interests. Their control of the medieval town empowered them to adapt its superstructure to the requirements of productive development.

> In the financial sphere, the towns organized taxation, finances, police order, customs and excise. They invented public loans. . . . One after another, they reinvented gold money. . . . They organized industry and the guilds; they invented long distance trade, bills of exchange, the first forms of trading companies and accountancy.[17]

Nor was this premonition of economic progress merely a false promise. The general crisis of the fourteenth century, writes Anderson, "was surmounted by a recombination of production factors in which for the first time specifically *urban* technological advances played the leading role."[18] Artillery, ocean navigation and printing were the three great technological innovations of the late medieval epoch; seaborne commerce eventually enabled Western Europe to conquer world supremacy.[19]

The process of formation of the bourgeoisie was given a powerful impetus by the rise of the absolutist state. Marx characterized absolutism as the result of an equilibrium between the declining feudal nobility and the nascent class of merchants. The special product of a historical transition, the centralized monarchy was able for a time to detach itself from the contending classes, and independently arbitrate between them.[20] This conception could even drift so far as to portray the late medieval state as the instrument of emerging bourgeois rule.[21] Other texts are more nuanced, presenting the absolute monarchy as the institutional framework within which feudal society sought to preserve itself. To be sure, this framework advanced the interests of the nascent bourgeoisie; yet its internal composition reflected the continued predominance of feudal class power—hence the necessity for the bourgeois revolutions.[22]

Marx assigned the absolutist state a progressive historical role due to its innovations in centralizing political rule.[23] The Crown, to be sure, began the process of suppressing the independence of the towns. The distinctive action of urban capitalism, however, manifested itself in all the institutions of absolutism. Indeed, the centralized monarchy reproduced the political superstructure pioneered by the towns on a national scale: it developed a uniform legal system, national taxation, the professional army, a permanent bureaucracy, underwrote the development of capital cities which anchored spreading commercial networks, and began to suppress the internal barriers to trade—all preeminently modern characteristics.

More significantly, the existing social relations of production and the corresponding legal and political superstructure were particularly well suited to the development of the productive forces. The centralized monarchy was the greatest single consumer in the country. It was overwhelmingly organized for war, which typically absorbed between two-thirds and four-fifths of its budget.[24] This military demand promoted the development of a whole new complex of industries—armaments, shipbuilding, metallurgy, gunpowder, leather—and stimulated the manufacture of consumer goods to provision troops—food, drink, clothing, shoes, and so on. Yet the government rarely adopted the role of direct producer in the late-medieval economy, typically relying on privately operated concerns. Financiers and merchants, particularly those specializing in seaborne commerce, were thus offered unprecedented profit opportunities by the Crown: they furnished the supplies necessary for the conduct of war. The capital investment required to raise the new industries was encouraged and assisted by state loans, subsidies, contracts and various kinds of privileges: The state granted the monopolies which offered essential protection to nascent capital by providing a guaranteed market for a given period of time.

The other side of the government's expenditures was its constant need for revenues. The requirements of public finance often dictated the Crown's economic policy. The main weight of royal taxes fell on the peasant poor; the aristocracy was in effect always exempt from taxation. The monarchy's ambitious expansionist policies would therefore always find it short of funds. This situation, again, provided lucrative business opportunities for the urban bourgeoisie. The great bankers and financiers had grown up in the service of the Crown; their chief business was making government loans and farming the indirect taxes. Trade, especially overseas commerce, could also yield a significant income to the monarch. Like the financiers, merchants were an important source of credit to the state; tariffs and customs duties, often farmed out to wealthy individuals, raised considerable revenues. Above all, however, the sale of monopoly rights in a special branch of trade became a means of solving the government's fiscal problems.

Another expedient to which monarchs resorted in their quest for revenues involved the sale of offices in the royal bureaucracy. Extensively developed in France, this practice made sound political sense: it provided the Crown with an indispensable weapon in overcoming the centrifugal pull of aristocratic particularism. Its main beneficiaries, however, were men of recent bourgeois extraction, who had made their fortune through trade and commerce. Similarly, Henry VIII's confiscation of Church property was largely designed to enhance royal power and provide the Crown with an economic base independent of the nobility. Its sale to pay for war, however, greatly strengthened and commercialized the landed gentry.

In sum, the absolutist state and the nascent bourgeoisie formed a symbiotic relationship—a mutually beneficial association between two historically dissimilar entities. The field of compatibility between their interests found expression in mercantilism, the ruling doctrine of the epoch. Perhaps one of the clearest expressions of mercantilism was the emergence of wars motivated by commercial ambitions, an essentially novel phenomenon that became the hallmark of the seventeenth century.[25] Its historical significance lay in the fact that it created some of the essential prerequisites of capitalist modernization:[26] The monarchy promoted capital investment in new industry because it was necessary for the successful conduct of its policy of war and magnificence; the mercantile and manufacturing bourgeoisie developed a precocious mass production, pioneering methods of concentrating and rationalizing the work process. The state encouraged trade because of its fiscal possibilities; the mercantile bourgeoisie laid the basis for a world market, organizing economic space and commodity circulation in a way that eventually permitted the emergence of the capitalist economy. The monarchy's constant need for revenues provided opportunities for the investment of usury capital; financiers, bankers and merchants amassed great concentrations of money wealth and developed procedures of accounting necessary for the rational conduct of business. The multiplication of public courts spawned various kinds of lawyers—judges, solicitors, notaries, barristers—who assumed responsibility for clarifying the prerogatives of the Crown and the nobility. At the same time, the lawyers not only began drafting a rational and unified system of law, but also brought to the fore a potentially self-conscious leadership for the nascent bourgeoisie. They would, indeed, furnish a great part of its revolutionary personnel.

Feudal Property Relations Fetter Productive Development

The absolute monarchy's progressive contribution to economic growth reached its limits at the barrier set by its conditions of existence. Insofar as the mercantile and manufacturing bourgeoisie maintained its subaltern relation to the Crown and left the peasant cultivators in their condition of dependence on the aristocracy, they were encouraged to develop the urban economy. The state's economic role became dysfunctional, however, when productive development permitted the bourgeoisie to extend its operations beyond the historical horizons of the ancien regime: Against the background of the ascendant commercial order, the Crown's policies assumed an increasingly regressive cast. For its part, the bourgeoisie began to experience the government's involvement in the economy as an ever more disruptive force, frustrating and falsifying its earlier promise for capital investment. Marx writes:

> Once society's material conditions of existence have developed so far that the transformation of its official political form has become a vital necessity for it, the whole physiognomy of the old political power is transformed. Thus absolute monarchy now attempts, not to centralise, which was its actual progressive function, but to decentralise. Born from the defeat of the feudal estates and having the most active share in their destruction itself, it now seeks to retain at least the semblance of feudal distinctions. Formerly encouraging trade and industry and thereby at the same time the rise of the bourgeois class, as necessary conditions both for national strength and for its own glory, absolute monarchy now everywhere hampers trade and industry, which have become increasingly dangerous weapons in the hands of an already powerful bourgeoisie. From the town, the birth-place of its rise to power, it turns its alarmed and by now dull glance to the countryside which is fertile with the corpses of its old powerful opponents.[27]

The system of monopolies, chartered companies, and guilds, which had provided the state with a critical source of revenue and materiel for its wars while offering nascent industries needed economic protection, increasingly fettered commercial and industrial growth by blocking the normal channels of trade and restricting output. Monopolies excluded the most progressive sectors of the bourgeoisie from participating in the expansion of the economy to the advantage of a favored few.[28] Obtainable mainly through court influence, they became a means by which courtiers enhanced their wealth and power rather than vehicles of economic development. The Cockayne Project, for example, proved disastrous for the majority of the English bourgeoisie. The monarchy's policy of military expansion, which had provided the main stimulus to the development of the age's most significant technical innovations, ultimately failed to further bourgeois interests. The French Crown's morbid interest in annexing territory was purchased at the expense of its maritime responsibilities: the price was paid by the merchants, who lost most of their colonies in North America and India. Yet even in England, whose relatively greater emphasis on naval warfare was conducive to the expansion of seaborne commerce, the monarchy had no concerted policy of advancing trade: it did not actively defend merchants against piracy or consistently support their struggle for markets against rival interests. The state's financial difficulties, which for so long had provided lucrative investment opportunities for usury capital, ultimately made the development of an orderly banking system impossible. The monarchy typically sought to reduce the crushing burden of debt by means—forced loans, devaluation of the currency, or outright repudiation or bankruptcy—which defrauded financial interests. Yet attempts at reform proved ruinous. The Law System, for example, in part an attempt to liberalize commerce and investment in eighteenth century France, plundered Parisian speculators.

Absolutism's fiscal deadlock, indeed, occasioned the crisis of governmental authority that precipitated the dismantling of the ancien regime. Unable to secure itself with an independent financial base, the Crown was compelled to impose a serious tax on the nobility and the bourgeoisie. The latter would agree, of course, only if allowed to assert some control over the state apparatus. Yet the proposal to reform the tax system raised the whole question of the nature and program of the absolutist state, and forced it to disclose and defend its class base: the monarchy closed ranks with the feudal interests of the country. The members of the bourgeoisie were thus thrown upon their own devices to grope their way towards independence. Marx writes:

> The bourgeois gentlemen . . . seek as far as possible to make the change from absolute to bourgeois monarchy without a revolution, in an amicable fashion.
>
> But the absolute monarchy . . . will not let itself be amicably changed into a bourgeois monarchy. It will not abdicate amicably. The princes' hands are tied both by their personal prejudices and by a whole bureaucracy of officials, soldiers and clerics—integral parts of absolute monarchy who are far from willing to exchange their ruling position for a subservient one in respect to the bourgeoisie. Then the feudal estates also hold back; for them it is a question of life or death, in other words, of property or expropriation. It is clear that the absolute monarch, for all the servile homage to the bourgeoisie, sees his true interest on the side of these estates.[29]

This hardening of interests created the logic that made the bourgeois revolutions necessary. Supported and propelled by commercial relations that facilitated continued material progress, the bourgeoisie disengaged itself from the fetters imposed by the traditional political framework. The revolutions provided the crucible that transformed its disparate and subordinate elements into a national ruling class.[30]

To summarize: Marx's positive evaluation of the merchants' contribution to the formation of capitalist class relations was grounded in his conception of their role in the commercial revolution that made possible an epochal development in society's productive forces. Merchants promoted the growth of the division of labor, both within and between nations, creating a national and then a world market. Engendered originally within "the feudal organization of trades," indeed protected by it, the new forces of production outstripped the limited possibilities for expansion that feudalism permitted. The discovery of the new trade routes in the sixteenth century gave a great impulse to economic progress. The system of handicrafts organized in guilds, corresponding to the division of labor between town and country, no longer sufficed to meet the increased scale of demand. Merchants thus began the process of seizing production from its feudal form. They lifted the labor process from the monopolistic restrictions of the towns by escaping to the country and organizing rural crafts in putting out industries. In this system, peasants and artisans were reduced to a position of dependence on the merchants who put out work for them to do, monopolizing the supply of raw materials and the sale of their finished products. Large numbers of direct producers were thus brought under the command of city merchants, progressively acquiring the characteristics of wage laborers. The putting out system, corresponding to the division of labor between towns, itself proved insufficient to meet the growing demand of a world market, and gradually gave way to the manufactory.[31]

These advances in the technical organization of labor empowered a ruling class whose members—bankers, merchants, manufacturers—possessed the requisite capacity and interest to sustain continued growth. The rise of this class, however, was increasingly frustrated by the old social order. Hence, the revolution.

> Privilege, the institution of guilds and corporations, the regulatory system of the Middle Ages, were the only social relations that corresponded to the acquired productive forces and to the pre-existing social conditions from which those institutions had emerged. Protected by the corporative and regulatory system, capital had accumulated, maritime trade had expanded, colonies had been founded—and man would have lost the very fruits of all this had he wished to preserve the forms under whose protection those fruits had ripened. And, indeed, two thunderclaps occurred, the revolutions of 1640 and of 1688. In England, all the earlier economic forms, the social relations corresponding to them, and the political system which was the official expression of the old civil society, were destroyed. . . . With the acquisition of new productive faculties man changes his mode of production and with the mode of production he changes all the economic relations which were but the necessary relations of that particular mode of production.[32]

THE LIMITS OF MERCHANT CAPITALISM

Marx's later works contain a series of historical investigations which sharply contradict his earlier positive estimate of the merchants' role in the transition to capitalism. Marx now characterizes as "wholly erroneous" the conception which traces the rise of capitalism to the commercial revolutions of the sixteenth and seventeenth centuries, its triumph actualizing the potential for productive development fettered by the continued dominance of the feudal regime.[33] Behind this reversal lies a shift in focus in which the expansion of markets and the material progress it facilitated are displaced by a class centered analysis. As we have seen, a class's contribution to economic growth is a by-product of the strategies its members are compelled to adopt to maximize the appropriation of surplus product. Accordingly, Marx's study seeks to explain not economic progress per se, but the *kind* of progress merchant capitalism promoted. He argues that merchants were essentially conservative: An investigation of the nexus between the operations of the mercantile bourgeoisie and the dominant feudal classes reveals that the continued accumulation of capital in its hands was dependent upon the continued effectiveness of the feudal mode of surplus appropriation. The type of growth made possible by merchant capitalism was therefore quite "incapable by itself of promoting and explaining the transition from one mode of production to another."[34] Quite the contrary, merchant capitalism was subject to the law of motion of the feudal economy. On the one hand, the progress of the productive forces it created depended upon and buttressed the preservation of the old order, and thus inhibited the rise of the new. On the other, the productive development to which it did contribute stalled and receded with the repeated crises that punctuated the decline of feudal society. Thus, if Marx earlier traced the emergence of capitalism to the activities of the mercantile bourgeoisie, he now underscored the merchants' resistance to it. The success of the capitalist mode of production, he concluded, presupposed the prior erosion of the merchants' power and independence.

The Sources of the Merchants' Profit

Merchant capitalism assumed a distinct historical existence when merchants succeeded in detaching the exchange of commodities from the system of production, establishing exclusive control over long-distance trade. The autonomy of the sphere of circulation was the necessary condition of their rise and the basis of their economic viability. Merchant capitalists extracted a surplus from trade or, more precisely, *by* trade, creating and exploiting disparities between the buying and selling price.[35] They thereby confined themselves, and remained confined, within the exchange process: the size of their profit margins depended upon their success in reserving the acts of buying and selling to themselves.[36]

These conditions of existence determined the strategies merchants adopted to maximize the appropriation of an economic surplus: they sought to expand their commercial operations and to tilt the terms of commerce in their favor, buying as cheaply and selling as dearly as possible.[37] These twin objectives were achieved by securing a monopoly of the carrying trade.[38] Given a rudimentary level of economic development, general conditions themselves created "natural" monopolies, permitting merchants to gather a surplus "by promoting the exchange of products of commercially and otherwise economically undeveloped societies."[39] Profits would be secured by taking advantage of the naturally given "difference between the prices of production of various countries."[40]

Society's economic progress, however, dissolved these natural profit opportunities. The saturation of existing markets, characteristic of the later Middle Ages, required merchants to revise their business strategies: they now sought to increase profits by artificial monopolies, capturing and enforcing exclusive control over markets and creating price disparities by deliberate design. This strategy comprised two interrelated tactics.[41] First, merchants sought to maximize the volume of trade coming their way by establishing commercial monopolies against competing merchants. This tactic depended upon their success in extending the political power of towns. Their chief aim was to usurp a privileged position as middlemen in the entrepôt trade. They ousted rivals from a given branch of commerce, thus obtaining sole dominance over it; they diverted commercial traffic into their own markets, arresting trade by compelling competitors to sell exclusively to them, thereby making themselves unavoidable links in the chain of commerce, and so on. These means were primarily "extraeconomic," involving piracy and retaliation, diplomacy and alliances, trade embargoes and outright armed struggle against rival merchants and towns.[42] Success ensured a monopoly of access to a given market, trade route, or some vital commodity.

Second, merchants sought to alter the terms of trade in their favor, that is, to buy cheaply and sell dearly, by establishing exclusive monopolies against consumers and producers. The success of this strategy presupposed control of the administrative apparatus of the towns, seized by restrictive companies of merchants as early as the thirteenth century.[43] On the one hand, political power was used to raise the prices of consumer goods merchants imported into the town. On the other hand, control of the town government was used to exclude craftsmen from the major trading guilds, in effect limiting their economic autonomy. Merchants organized the putting out system of industry by monopolizing the craftsmen's access to their raw materials, ensuring that producers obtained work solely from them, and the disposal of their finished goods, guaranteeing that producers sold exclusively to them. This system empowered merchants to maximize profit margins by forcing down the prices of production of the goods they exported. The restrictions imposed upon the craftsmen would sometimes extend so far as to forbid any collusion between them at different stages of the labor process, thereby preempting any entrepreneurial element amongst the craftsmen, particularly those employing labor, from acquiring control of production from within. Merchants also used political power more directly to regulate wages, hours and working conditions; "anticombination" laws sought to destroy or prohibit the formation of craftsmen or journeymen fraternities designed to raise prices or wages. The leading burgess groups in the towns would thus augment profits by depressing the economic conditions of existence of the direct producers.[44]

The Nature of Merchant Capitalism's Contribution to Economic Progress

Merchant capitalism flourishes as an independent economic force *outside* the prevailing mode of production: it interposes itself "between extremes it does not control, and between premises it does not create."[45] To be sure, it is thereby capable of intertwining historically diverse, even competing, systems of exploitation—slave, feudal, capitalist. The necessary condition of the merchants' capacity to accumulate capital is their exclusive control over the exchange of commodities, *regardless* of the basis upon which products are produced and appropriated.[46] But this means that the relationship between a producing and an appropriating class, which determines a society's internal dynamic, exists for merchants as *given*, external to their operations. Accordingly, they do not play a central role in a society's historical development; nor are they capable of promoting and explaining the supersession of one type of society by another.[47] Rather, merchant capitalists typically adjust themselves to the rhythm of the prevailing regime, parasitically drawing a profit from it.

In this view, then, there can be no immanent evolution from the precapitalist to the capitalist market, nor can the mercantile bourgeoisie be characterized as the linear precursor of the capitalist bourgeoisie.[48] On the contrary, "the independent development of merchant's capital," Marx argues, "is inversely proportional to the degree of development of capitalist production."[49] The distinguishing characteristic of the capitalist mode of production is that class relations themselves assume the form of exchange relations: labor power is bought and sold on the market as a commodity.[50] The supremacy of merchant capital, however, presupposes the separation of the sphere of circulation from the system of production. Merchant capital, therefore, typically flourished in precapitalist societies, where the contending classes had primarily nonmarket access to their means of subsistence and reproduction.[51]

To be sure, the strategies merchants adopted to maximize profits made some significant contributions to the development of society's productive forces. Their struggle to enhance the political power of the cities revolutionized the relationship between town and country, accelerating the division of labor and the specialization of economic activity. Their attempt to augment the volume of trade available to them promoted the organization of ever more extensive markets and led to the development of maritime commerce, ultimately giving Western Europe economic supremacy on a world scale. Their endeavor to increase price disparities by squeezing the direct producers induced them to develop a precocious mass production, concentrating and rationalizing the work process by organizing it on a putting out basis. Their policy of exploiting by trade permitted them to pool profits from disparate economic systems by manipulating their economic surpluses, concentrating wealth in the form of exchange value, the original historical form of capital—money circulating for the sole end of self-expansion.

Nevertheless, the *kind* of economic growth to which merchant capitalists contributed was always dependent on the economic dynamism of the mode of production whose demand they fulfilled and surplus they exchanged. The nature of their contribution to historical evolution, therefore, was very much a "dependent variable": Whether and to what extent they promoted the supersession of feudalism by capitalism was wholly dependent on the course of development and outcome of feudal class struggle.[52] The accumulation of merchant capital depended upon the level of productivity achieved by the society to which it attached itself.[53] Merchant capitalists gathered an economic surplus largely by redistributing wealth *after* it had been extracted from the producers, wealth they did little to generate. The renaissance of merchant capitalism in the Middle Ages was grounded in and sustained by a rise in rural vigor engendered by the feudal mode of production. The increasing size and disposability of seigneurial incomes were the necessary preconditions which fueled the expansion of international trade, the development of manufactories and the growth of big commercial and banking centers in medieval Europe: These occurrences, writes Hilton, "are chronologically secondary to the development of the forces of production in agriculture, stimulated by the process of the struggle for feudal rent."[54]

Feudal lords and merchants shared an objective interest with the nobility with respect to "the exploitation of the countryside so long as rent remained, in its various forms, the principal mode of appropriation and capital remained external to the productive process."[55] This is not to say that merchants and lords did not engage in bitter, often bloody, struggles. The history of the medieval world was rife with the conflict between town and country. Theirs was not, however, a class struggle. Rather, it reflected an intraclass rivalry between competing segments of the same regime:

> This conflict concerned the disposal of the surplus over subsistence and re-production needs which the ruling class claimed from the basic producers. The conflict between feudal lords and urban patriciates, through the mediating chain of commercial and political relationships, concerned the share-out of the surplus once it had been taken from the basic producers.[56]

Medieval agriculture, like precapitalist agriculture in general, imposed strict limits on the development of urban manufacture.[57] The household economy of peasants was in the main self-sufficient. Moreover, most peasant households had little surplus to sell after the lords' exactions. Whatever surplus they did retain was chiefly devoted to the purchase of land, not producer or consumer goods.[58] The peasants' limited demand precluded the development of a mass home market for inexpensive goods capable of being mass produced by mechanizing and concentrating the work process. What demand for urban industry existed typically arose from the lords' expenditures for luxury items or the monarchy's outlays for strategic and administrative ends. The demand for luxury goods, however, had only a limited importance for general economic progress. Luxury production, by its very nature, "depends upon hand skills, not on machinery; what is sought by the customer is individual excellence in the product, not cheapness or utility."[59] Government contracts designed to serve the Crown's policy of war and magnificence did tend to encourage large scale production. But these enterprises were typically artificial creations: they did not initiate a process of economic expansion.[60]

Marx maintained that the relationship between merchants and craftsmen paralleled the relationship between lords and serfs. Merchant capitalists exploited urban industry by feudal means, reproducing the rural organization of surplus extraction inside the town.[61] The craftsmen, like the peasant cultivators, typically possessed their own means of production. The basic economic unit in both town and country, the artisan's workshop and the peasant's holding, was based on the family's labor force, with seldom more than two or three hired hands. The peasant village had its counterpart in the guilds that tightly regulated the town's division of labor and the distribution of the main occupational strata—masters, apprentices, journeymen—within the workshop.[62] Thus, like the peasant villages, the urban craft guilds were quite capable of independently organizing economic life without the intervention of any ruling class. Both merchant and lord, therefore, were compelled to extract a surplus from the direct producers through extraeconomic—that is, juridical and political—coercion: "The merchants established fields of activity for which they obtained sanction from the feudal authorities in the form of monopolies and privileges."[63]

The merchants' control over craftsmen in the putting out system was essentially different from the capitalists' control over outwork common in the eighteenth and nineteenth centuries. The merchants left production largely in the hands of the craftsmen, permitting them to retain their artisanal status and institutions. They rarely penetrated the sphere of production itself, organizing it to manufacture goods on their own account. The putting out system, in fact, "turned out to be the appropriate form for controlling production without a direct involvement in it."[64] It represented mainly a development of craft production for international markets. The buyers of the merchants' commodities, luxuries especially, were persons whose incomes came from the revenues of their landed property—that is, the nobility and the clergy.

The craftsmen, for their part, jealously guarded the traditions of their trade. They regarded their skill or "mystery" as their primary property. The guilds enforced the regulations that protected this property by restricting entry into a trade through complex apprenticeship requirements, fixing production quotas, delaying the introduction of new products and technologies, setting quality standards and prices, and so on. Their wages were determined less by economic considerations of supply and demand than by notions of social prestige and just price.

The contradiction inherent in merchant capital's accumulation process was in essence a feudal contradiction. That is, merchants tended to wrest more surplus from industry than they returned to it in the form of productive investments.[65] The widening of the merchants' profit margins depended on their capacity to appropriate a surplus from direct producers who were potentially independent of them, over whom they exercised political power, but with respect to whom they played only a limited entrepreneurial role. Accordingly, the accumulation of commercial capital was not conditional upon industrial expansion. Indeed, merchants were little interested in productive investments.[66] The most rational avenue available to them to increase profit margins was by buying, not producing, as cheaply as possible, and their class position empowered them to do so by squeezing the craftworkers. Thus, merchant capital eventually impaired its economic base, undermining the capacity of industry to maintain material life.

> In point of fact, [the] merchant . . . let the [craftsmen] carry on in their old unorganised way and exerted only a merchant's control, for that was for whom they really worked. This system presents everywhere an obstacle to the real capitalist mode of production and goes under with its development. Without revolutionising the mode of production, it only worsens the condition of the direct producers, turns them into mere wage-workers and proletarians under conditions worse than those under the immediate control of capital, and appropriates their surplus-labour on the basis of the old mode of production.[67]

In sum, the operations of merchant capital were closely dependent upon the nature and program of the feudal regime.[68] The economic impulse merchants carried from the countryside to the city generated little pressure for productive innovation in urban industry, which assumed an essentially parasitic and conservative character. The impulse they carried back to the countryside exerted an equally weak economic stimulus: merchants transported few goods, such as means of production, which enhanced rural productivity.

THE SEVENTEENTH CENTURY CRISIS

Merchant capitalism's subaltern dependence on the feudal mode of production determined its historical horizons: the productive forces it created waxed and waned with the rise and decline of the old regime. The general crisis of the seventeenth century revealed the limits of the merchants' contribution to economic growth. The study of this period is fraught with controversy. It is generally agreed that seventeenth century Europe experienced a crisis, but little agreement exists regarding the nature and locus of the crisis complex. For E. J. Hobsbawm, who launched the scholarly debate, the crisis was in essence an economic one, and its significance lay in the fact that it irreparably impaired the feudal mode of production, clearing the way for an unprecedented consolidation of capitalism.[69] This thesis has been sharply challenged, primarily on the ground that the pattern of economic trends in the seventeenth century is in such disarray.[70] T. K. Rabb, following a lengthy review of the controversy, reached the conclusion that "it is time to admit that the larger case [for a 'crisis' interpretation] cannot rest on evidence from [the economic] quarter."[71] Yet curiously, two pages later he asserts that

> there is no denying that, in contrast to both the sixteenth and eighteenth centuries, just about every locality in Europe suffered a major setback, with serious consequences, at some time during the seventeenth century.

He then explains:

> On the larger canvas the changes are unmistakable. The influx of precious metals slumped precipitously. . . . The yield of crops dropped in the seventeenth century for the first time since the late Middle Ages. . . . [A]ll indices, whether of prices, industrial and agricultural production, or trade, reveal a transition from boom to stagnation following the well-nigh universal economic crisis around 1619–1622. At the same time the flight to the cities, with their dreadful mortality; the hardships of vagrancy; and the steady emigration overseas; all accentuated the slackening of population growth at the aggregate level. . . . The signs of hard times are inescapable.[72]

To be sure, Hobsbawm's view that the seventeenth century crisis amounted to a "fundamental . . . solution of the difficulties which had previously stood in the way of the triumph of capitalism" must be amended.[73] It seems clear that the crisis complex was not one in which a set of progressive productive forces clashed against an unproductive and wasteful feudal regime, occasioning a series of changes leading toward capitalist production. The mercantile bourgeoisie did not mature within an enclave in feudal society, eventually expanding beyond feudalism's conditions of existence, but as an integral part of it, wholly dependent on the ruling classes and state power. Accordingly, the crisis did not result in the rise of capital accumulation, but in the decline and involution of commercial capital away from investment in shipping and manufacture towards rentier, that is, *feudal,* forms of wealth.[74] This is not to deny, however, that the locus of the crisis complex was in the economy. Rather, the Marxian thesis of the dynamics of crisis in a mode of production can be rescued if it is properly revised: The historical evidence points to a contraction—not a breakthrough—of the productive forces within the prevailing relations of production. The seventeenth century did not witness the end of feudalism, but an alteration of its dominant class relations. What emerged was not an early form of capitalism, but centralized feudalism, anchored by the absolutist state.

In this view, the absolutist state provided the central institution around which the nobility regrouped in its struggle to arrest the erosion of its class power at the hands of the peasantry following the fourteenth century crisis. This is the conclusion of a generation of Marxist historians, summarized by Anderson: "Absolutism was essentially just this: a redeployed and recharged apparatus of feudal domination, designed to clamp the peasant masses back into their traditional social position—despite and against the gains they had won by the widespread commutation of dues."[75]

The seventeenth century was the period during which the absolutist state consolidated its power, forging the administrative structure that permitted the nobility to continue its passive existence on surplus extracted from the peasantry by extra-economic means.[76] Under its aegis, the economic privileges of lordship were reconstituted, although its political and military prerogatives were gathered up within the machinery of the state. That is, absolutism preserved the nobility's economic base, but at a price, namely, a transfer of the lords' private rights of jurisdiction "upward" to the public jurisdiction of the Crown.[77] A national system of justice, superimposed on the seigneurial courts, now assumed primary responsibility for providing the legal support, ultimately backed by the monarch's superior military force, which empowered the lords to command and thus exploit the land and labor of dependent peasant cultivators. The centralized monarchy was organized to repress peasant rebellions and control wages and the mobility of labor by national regulation. A national system of extraeconomic coercion siphoned from the peasant economy the revenues necessary to finance the monarchy's policy of war and magnificence: royal taxes represented a form of "centralized feudal rent" overlaying the "local feudal rent" levied at the manorial level. At the same time, the monarchy drew the nobility to itself by means of the offices it made available in both the military and civilian apparatus, and the largess of its court. In sum, the absolutist state represented "the new political carapace of a threatened nobility."[78]

This conception of the centralized monarchy's class base permits an economic reinterpretation of the crisis: The European economy as a whole underwent a period of contraction in the seventeenth century, first in Spain and Italy, and then in Northern France and the Netherlands. Yet it did not, as in the fourteenth century, experience a general retrogression; rather, this was a "multilayered" crisis, even in its socioeconomic aspects, striking different parts of Europe at different times and different sectors of the economy with different degrees of intensity.[79] The epoch is characterized by a dramatic shift in the economic center of gravity in Europe from the Mediterranean, which was quickly on the way to becoming an economic backwater by mid-century, to the North Sea, which witnessed a spectacular rise in commercial activity.[80] Moreover, although it is clear that agricultural production passed through a serious depression, long-term trends in the urban economy are less clear.[81] If Italy's trade and manufacture declined, Holland's flourished.

In what sense, then, can the seventeenth century be understood as an epoch of crisis for merchant capitalism? How can this "general crisis" be made to square with urban prosperity?[82] An answer is suggested if attention is focused not on the fact of prosperity per se, but on the *kind* of prosperity experienced by the urban economy. For lying concealed behind the development of commerce and industry was a reorientation of urban capital towards a closer accommodation with the prevailing regime.[83] That is, it is difficult to avoid the impression that the mercantile bourgeoisie was able to weather the rural depression only to the extent that it adjusted its interests to the needs of the old order, accepting its limitations and learning to live parasitically off it. Insofar as the monarchy and the nobility succeeded in continuing to extract a surplus from the rural producers, their demand would shelter the commodity sector from the full impact of the agricultural slump.[84] Urban capital, for its part, could readily adjust its interests to the monarchy and the nobility, for it posed no threat to their hold on the countryside—the basis of their power. Since the means whereby it appropriated a surplus did not rest on mass production, its continued accumulation did not per se require a radical rupture with the feudal agrarian order—the future labor and consumer market of capitalism—which still contained the vast majority of the dependent peasant population.[85]

This dynamic might help explain the course of development of the crisis.[86] Given the absence of a reorganization of the countryside, a specialized urban center could avoid the ravages of depression, or even prosper in its midst, to the extent that it succeeded in monopolizing the entrepôt trade of the entire continent, and in adapting itself to the luxury market and to the administrative and strategic needs of the state. It could thereby pool the profits gathered from various economic regions. Yet its adaptation to the feudal mode of production could not, of course, ensure continuous prosperity; given its failure to develop an adequate home base for capital accumulation, it only postponed the evil day.[87] The Italian "Indian summer" of the second half of the sixteenth century, built on a monopoly of foreign markets, gave way to a long-term decline beginning around 1600.[88] The Netherlands' "golden age," achieved in spite of—or perhaps, more accurately, at the expense of—the decline and turmoil witnessed in the rest of Europe, which permitted Dutch shipping to establish a hegemony of the world carrying trade, began to tarnish around the mid-seventeenth century, when it was at last overtaken by the general economic contraction.[89] The French urban economy began to recover from its midcentury slump around 1660 under the aegis of the absolutist state—this was the epoch of Colbert—by shifting to the production of luxuries and for the needs of the monarchy, thereby ensuring for itself a parasitic existence for another century and a half.[90] The price was an agricultural economy that showed increasing "signs of maturity, sclerosis and fatigue" throughout the seventeenth century, entering a process of irreversible decline after 1675–1680.[91] Only England, as we shall see in the next chapter, witnessed the qualitative transformation of the feudal class structure which made possible self-sustaining economic growth.[92]

When the general crisis reached the urban centers, nothing revealed more clearly the position of merchant capitalists as a fraction of the feudal ruling class than their response: the merchants typically redirected their capital away from urban production towards "proprietary" forms of wealth.[93] That is, they did not emancipate themselves from their subservience to the old regime, nor did they establish an independent home base in industry. Rather, urban capital recuperated its losses by exploiting the profit opportunities offered by the agrarian economy and the emerging public sector. Needless to say, its influx into land did not signal the appearance of capitalist modes of investment in the countryside. On the contrary, the whole weight of the urban bourgeoisie was directed toward preserving seigneurial levies and obligations, rationalizing and tightening the interlocking complex of extraeconomic means whereby a surplus was extracted from the dependent peasant cultivators. The new landlords simply introduced the business practices learned in the town into the management of seigneurie. Accordingly, the flight of urban wealth into the countryside was normally accompanied by a seigneurial reaction.[94]

Capital investment in the public economy created by the feudal state was yet another way in which the mercantile bourgeoisie accommodated itself to the old regime: wealth escaping the economic slump in the towns sought safe havens in venal offices, tax farming, state loans, *rentes*, annuities, and so on. Its effect was to forestall and erect barriers to the emergence of capitalist social relations. Referring to French developments, but with implications which are general in scope, Anderson writes:

> The purchase of offices represented such a profitable investment that capital was perpetually diverted away from manufacturing or mercantile ventures into a usurious collusion with the Absolutist State. Sinecures and fees, tax-farms and loans, honours and bonds all drew bourgeois wealth away from production. The acquisition of noble titles and

fiscal immunity became normal entrepreneurial goals for *roturiers*. The social consequence was to create a bourgeoisie which tended to become increasingly assimilated to the aristocracy itself, via exemptions and privileges of offices. The State, in its turn, sponsored royal manufactures and public trading companies which, from Sully to Colbert, provided business outlets for this class. The result was to "side-track" the political evolution of the French bourgeoisie for a hundred and fifty years.[95]

If the feudal ruling class cushioned the impact of the economic contraction upon the city, it precipitated it in the countryside. Indeed, like its predecessor in the fourteenth century, the general crisis of the seventeenth century was a crisis of the internal mechanisms of reproduction of the feudal mode of production.[96] Their outward aspects were similar—ecological imbalance gave over to demographic exhaustion. Population growth in the sixteenth century had led to the cultivation of increasingly marginal lands; agricultural yield ratios stabilized and then fell. Sometime during the seventeenth century the movement of land reclamation came to a halt and began to contract. Demographic expansion tipped into overpopulation at the first stroke of harvest failure—there were three in the mid-seventeenth century, the worst in 1649–1650. Population fell, as famine and its accompanying Horsemen—pestilence, disease, and war—took their toll. Clearly, this was a "crisis of subsistence," typical of precapitalist social formations, not a "crisis of overproduction," characteristic of capitalist social formations.

The roots of the crisis lay in the contradiction between the ways in which the members of the ruling class were obliged to use their economic resources to preserve their position as rulers on the one hand, and the need to allocate resources to refurbish society's productive base on the other. The typical expenditures of the feudal ruling class did not make progressive contributions to the economy. In contrast to the thirteenth and fourteenth centuries, however, the fastest growing demands on the peasant economy came from the Crown, not the lords. The rural population experienced an unprecedented rise in the fiscal pressure exerted by the state, which devoted the overwhelming portion of its revenues towards military ends.[97] This meant that the monarchy pumped out an increasing share of the surplus product of the direct producers, but returned little of it in the form of investments which would increase production. The result was a progressive paralysis in the capacity of the rural economy to reproduce material life.[98] Like its predecessor, the seventeenth century crisis unleashed desperate peasant rebellions, particularly directed against the fiscal agents of the Crown.[99] But the absolutist state now revealed its efficacy: If the fourteenth century peasantry succeeded in loosening the grip of aristocratic domination, the seventeenth century feudal state battened mercilessly on the rural population, brutally depressing the cultivators' economic conditions of life.[100]

In this class struggle, the town (or at least substantial elements in it) weighed in on the side of the ruling class: On the one hand, the size of the commodity sector was of critical importance to the state's political and military strength; on the other, the resources transferred by the state to the city permitted it to avoid the worst of the agricultural slump. Far from representing the promise of an entirely new epoch in human history, the mercantile bourgeoisie closed ranks with the feudal aristocracy.

THE GENESIS OF THE INDUSTRIAL CAPITALIST: TWO PATHS

Marx suggests that the transition to capitalist forms of industrial organization followed two major paths. According to the first, "the producer becomes merchant and capitalist, in contrast to the natural agricultural economy and the guild-bound handicrafts of the medieval urban industries." According to the second, "the merchant establishes direct sway over production." The first "is the really revolutionising path." The second, although serving "historically as a stepping-stone . . . cannot by itself contribute to the overthrow of the old mode of production, but tends rather to preserve and retain it as its precondition."[101]

Way number one refers to the origins of capitalist industry: its initial impulse, Marx indicates, came from within the ranks of the small producers. Way number two refers to merchant capitalism's contribution to productive development. Marx emphasizes that there was no linear evolution from merchant capitalism to capitalist industry; nor were the two ways simply alternative paths to the same end. Rather, ways number one and number two are contradictory, belonging, so to speak, to qualitatively different modes of production.

The success of merchant capitalism depended on its accommodation with the feudal order. Its role in foreign trade had been "prominent in the medieval economy for hundreds of years without significantly transforming it."[102] The emergence of capitalist industry presupposed the prior dissolution of the merchants' supremacy. The conflict between them is reflected in the respective fates of Holland and England in the seventeenth century. These years were "the high noon of merchant capitalism" in both countries. But its very triumph in Holland blocked the development of capitalist manufacturing.[103] "The history of the decline of Holland as the ruling trading nation," wrote Marx, "is the history of the subordination of merchant's capital to industrial capital."[104]

Capitalist accumulation, Marx argues, had its origins within the ranks of the petty producers, among careful small investors who accumulated family or group savings and began pulling themselves up by their own bootstraps, plowing their profits back into industry.[105] Specifically, Marx identifies the inception of capitalist production in a process of economic differentiation among the urban producers. Successful small masters slowly expanded the scope of their operations by retaining and developing a position as employers, reducing to wage labor both the less fortunate masters within their own ranks and the journeymen who already formed a large propertyless proletariat in most large early modern towns. This was way number one. The question of the rise of capitalist industry in the city is thus the question of the circumstances that gave rise to this process of differentiation.

The answer lies in the outcome of the class struggle between merchants and craftsmen. Their conflict normally assumed two forms: a struggle by the craftsmen to gain greater access to the regulatory apparatus of the guilds, or to incorporate in associations of their own, which could defend their separate interests. The merchants, for their part, sought to maintain control of those guilds to which traders and producers belonged jointly, to prevent the formation of new craft guilds, or to weaken their power where they already existed.

This class struggle sharply checked the process of economic differentiation among the direct producers. On the one hand, the putting out system prevented the masters from expanding production by impairing their ability to save and invest, and by restricting their opportunity to purchase raw materials more directly and cheaply. On the other, the divisions within the ranks of the craftsmen themselves were always circumscribed by their need to defend common interests against the encroachments of the merchants, limiting the craftsmen's ability to raise profits by increasing the number of apprentices and journeymen they employed. The requirements of class struggle provided one of the main motivating forces behind the cohesiveness of the craft guilds.[106] Thus, although the guilds, like the peasant communities, were by no means associations of equals, their internal stratification was always closely circumscribed by the need to defend common interests against the dominant merchant class: "One thing which always bound together all grades of craftsmen was the demand that old policies should be reversed so that all could buy and sell freely."[107]

The transition to capitalism in the cities presupposed the *prior* dissolution of the feudal organization of industry. This disintegration, however, was obviously not the product of the mercantile bourgeoisie pushing its way to independence within the interstices of the old regime, for the continued accumulation of merchant capital depended upon feudal relations of exploitation. Rather, the feudal class nexus in the towns unraveled from within, as a result of the petty producers' struggle against the system of mercantile control of industry. The revolt of the small craftsmen irreparably damaged the complex of extraeconomic coercion whereby the merchants wrested a surplus from them. It is *this* struggle, inherent in the feudal mode of production, that is principally responsible for the decline of the old order.

The emancipation of the small producers from feudal exploitation, Marx suggests, gave rise to the accumulation of capital in industry. For, ironically, the very success of the craftsmen's struggle for emancipation occasioned their own disintegration as a class. Thus, under certain circumstances, the parallel between the craft guilds and the peasant communities extended to the logic of their historical fate: When the grip of merchant capital over production lost its strength, the craftsmen's solidarity began to dissolve, and the guilds in the larger urban centers threw up an entrepreneurial element that propelled industry on to a capitalist path. On the one hand, small masters were now able both to retain their savings and use them more rationally, plowing back profits to increase production. On the other, the craft guilds lost their rationale and began to dissolve. The wealthier master craftsmen captured their regulatory apparatus and transformed it into an employers' tool, forcing their less successful brethren, apprentices, and journeymen to proletarian status. Alternatively, the new entrepreneurs accelerated the migration of production to the countryside, where they developed the productive potential of the putting out system.[108]

The process of differentiation among the direct producers eventually found expression in a new class struggle centered around a new axis: the division between merchant and craftworker gave way to a growing rift between the masters and their employees. As the guild structure decayed or became the sole preserve of employers, the journeymen and wage laborers began to form their own associations to protect their own wages and working conditions. In this struggle, the employment of rural labor was one of the principal means of destroying the independence of the artisans and reducing them to the status of wage laborers. The ready availability of rural labor eroded the position of urban artisans, who fought a losing struggle to maintain and enforce apprenticeship regulations. Indeed, rural outworkers were typically employed in the simpler production processes. More highly skilled operations, especially in the quality trades, remained in the hands of urban craftsmen. Thus, in sharp contrast to mercantile control over outwork, capitalist control over outwork predominated in those industries which had wholly lost their artisanal status. Their chief products were the cheap and ready commodities destined for a mass market.[109]

The expropriation of the craftsmen opened the way for the

triumph of capitalist industry. The new class of masters transformed the relationship between employers and laborers. The most bitter grievances of the urban artisans derived from the nature of the changes in the character of exploitation: the masters' abandonment of any lingering obligations toward their workers, of deference to their status, independence, or the customary traditions of their craft, of responsibility for offering a fair wage.[110] Marx refers to this process, which consolidated capitalist class relations, as the "formal subjection" of labor to capital. This process preceded, indeed, it was the indispensable precondition for, labor's "real subjection" to capital—that is, its subordination to capitalist industrialization.[111]

In the final analysis, however, Marx emphasizes that the central dynamic which impelled the transition from feudalism to capitalism was not played out in the city, but in the countryside. The extent of economic differentiation within the ranks of the urban producers depended upon the nature and composition of the rural economy. Given the overwhelming preponderance of agriculture in precapitalist societies, the degree of prosperity the countryside was capable of achieving strictly determined the possibilities for urban development. The prior growth of agricultural productivity prepared the way for industrial advance by permitting the gradual release of the factors of production, especially labor power, into industry and commerce, and by creating a home market for industrial products.[112]

NOTES

1. Marx, *The Poverty of Philosophy*, in Marx and Engels, Vol. 6 of *Collected Works*, pp. 185–86,(Hereafter *CW*.) Marx, Vol. 1 of *Capital*, p. 667. See also Dobb, *Studies in the Development of Capitalism*, pp. 177–80.

2. See Marx, *The German Ideology*, *CW* 5:64–74; *Manifesto of the Communist Party*, *CW* 6:485–89; and *The Poverty of Philosophy*, *CW* 6:175–76, 185–86. The transforming power of commerce and its impact on productive development plays a central role in G. A. Cohen's interpretation of historical materialism. See *Karl Marx's Theory of History*, pp. 298–302.

3. Marx, *Capital* 3:323–37 (Ch. 20) and 593–613 (Ch. 36) examines the mercantile and banking bourgeoisie; *Capital* 1:667–712 (Part 8), deals with the transitional dynamics in the countryside. See also Marx, *Grundrisse*, pp. 504–14.

4. Smith, *The Wealth of Nations* Book 1, Chs. 1–4 and Book 3, Chs. 1, 3 and 4; Steuart, Vol. 1 of *An Inquiry into the Principles of Political Economy,* Book 1, Chs. 6, 10 and 20, and Book 2, Ch. 13. Robert Brenner provides an excellent analysis of the theoretical presuppositions of this tradition of economic historiography. See "The Social Basis of Economic Development," in Roemer, ed., *Analytical Marxism,* pp. 23–53. See also, Brenner, "The Origins of Capitalist Development," pp. 25–92.

5. See in particular Weber, *The City*, pp. 80–89, 93–96, 102–14, 186–92, 212–13, 222–24. And Weber, *General Economic History*, pp. 92–111, 274–78, 315–51.

6. See: Pirenne, *Economic and Social History of Medieval Europe*, pp. 41–56, 77–85, 160–166, 206–19; *Medieval Cities,* Chs. 6–8; *A History of Europe*, Book 9; and *The Stages in the Social History of Capitalism*, pp. 1–22.

7. See "A Critique," and "A Rejoinder," in Hilton, ed., *The Transition From Feudalism to Capitalism*, pp. 33–56 and 102–08.

8. Wallerstein, Vol. 1 of *The Modern World System*, pp. 18–21, 67–129; "From Feudalism to Capitalism," 273–83; Wallerstein, "The Rise and Future Demise of the World Capitalist System," pp. 387–415. Braudel, *The Structures of Everday Life*, pp. 479–558. And *The Wheels of Commerce*, pp. 231–457.

9. Hibbert, "The Origins of the Medieval Town Patriciate," pp. 15–27; Hilton, "A Comment," in *The Transition From Feudalism to Capitalism,* pp. 109–11. Debate concerning Weber's theory of the transition has typically focused on a (often sterile) discussion of the role of ideas in history, a result of the prominence given to *The Protestant Ethic.* Weber's treatment of the role of towns and commerce as an essential condition underlying the emergence of modern capitalism in postfeudal Europe has elicited relatively little attention. For discussions of the substantive issues dividing Marx and Weber on the rise of capitalism, see Giddens, *Capitalism and Modern Social Theory*, pp. 178–80, 185–216; and *The Class Structure of the Advanced Societies*, pp. 45–52.

10. See, for example, Dobb, "A Reply," "A Further Comment," and "From Feudalism to Capitalism," pp. 57–67, 98–101, and 165–69; Takahashi, "A Contribution to the Discussion," pp. 68–97; Hilton, "Introduction," A Comment," and "Capitalism—What's in a Name?", pp. 9–29, 109–17, and 145–58. These articles appear in Hilton, ed., *The Transition From Feudalism to Capitalism.*

11. Brenner, "The Origins of Capitalist Development," pp. 29–33, 53–67; Elizabeth Fox-Genovese and Eugene D. Genovese, *Fruits of Merchant Capital*, pp. 187–93.

12. Marx, Letter to Engels, 27 July 1854, *CW* 39:473–76; *The German Ideology*, *CW* 5:34–35, 64–66. Cf. Weber, *General Economic History*, pp. 315–20, and *The City*, pp. 102–114; Pirenne, *Economic and Social History of Medieval Europe*, pp. 41–56; Braudel, *The Structures of Everyday Life*, pp. 509–14. See also Anderson, *Passages From Antiquity to Feudalism*, pp. 150–51.

13. Postan, *The Medieval Economy and Society*, p. 212.

14. Marx, *The German Ideology*, *CW* 5:67.

15. On the impact of the urban economy on class relations in the countryside, see Marx, *Economic and Philosophic Manuscripts of 1844*, *CW* 3:266–270, and *The German Ideology*, *CW* 5:64–65, 68–69, 79. Cf. Smith, *The Wealth of Nations*, pp. 507–20; Weber, *General Economic History*, pp. 92–111, and *The City*, pp. 190–92; Pirenne, *Economic and Social History of Medieval Europe*, pp. 77–85, and *A History of Europe*, pp. 532–36; Sweezy, "A Critique," in *The Transition From Feudalism to Capitalism*, ed. Rodney Hilton, pp. 41–46; Wallerstein, Vol. 1 of *The Modern World System*, pp. 87–116; Braudel, *The Wheels of Commerce*, pp. 264–65, 280–84, 294–97.

16. Marx, *The German Ideology*, *CW* 5:64–74, 76–77, and *Manifesto of the Communist Party*, *CW* 6:485–489. Cf. Weber, *The City*, pp. 212–13, 220–24; Pirenne, *Economic and Social History of Medieval Europe*, pp. 49–56, 100–166; Braudel, *The Structures of Everyday Life*, pp. 512–14, and *The Wheels of Commerce*, pp. 21–27, 232–43.

17. Braudel, *The Structures of Everyday Life*, p. 512. See also Marx, *The German Ideology*, *CW* 5:64.

18. Anderson, *Lineages of the Absolutist State*, p. 22.

19. Braudel provides an exhaustive discussion of these innovations: see, *The Structures of Everyday Life*, pp. 385–435. Cf. Anderson, *Lineages of the Absolutist State*, p. 22, n. 11.

20. Marx, "Moralising Criticism and Critical Morality," *CW* 6:326.

21. Marx, *Manifesto of the Communist Party*, *CW* 6:486.

22. See, for example, Marx, *The Eighteenth Brumaire of Louis Bonaparte*, *CW* 11:185–86. Anderson provides a brief survey of the different characterizations of absolutism by Marx and Engels: see *Lineages*, pp. 15–16 and 23, n. 12.

23. Marx, *The Eighteenth Brumaire of Louis Bonaparte*, *CW* 11:185–186; *The Civil War in France*, in *The Marx-Engels Reader*, pp. 629–30; "Moralising Criticism and Critical Morality," *CW* 6:319. Cf. Weber, *General Economic History*, pp. 334–51; Pirenne, *Economic and Social His-

tory of Medieval Europe, pp. 206–19; Sweezy, "A Rejoinder," in *The Transition From Feudalism to Capitalism*, ed. R. Hilton, pp. 107–08; Wallerstein, *The Modern World System* 1:87, 157–62, 225–97; Braudel, *The Structures of Everyday Life*, pp. 510, 527–31, and *The Wheels of Commerce*, pp. 514–55. See also Anderson, *Lineages*, pp. 17, 22–29, 39–41; and Theodore K. Rabb, *The Struggle for Stability in Early Modern Europe*, pp. 60–73, 92, 97–98.

24. For discussions of the centralized monarchy's economic policies and their impact, see sources listed in note 23. See also Hill, *Reformation to Industrial Revolution*, pp. 72–108; Hill, *The Century of Revolution*, pp. 15–17, 21–33; Clarkson, *The Pre-Industrial Economy in England*, pp. 159–209; Kemp, *Economic Forces in French History*, pp. 30–81; Pierre Goubert, *The Ancien Regime*, pp. 239–47; Georges Lefebvre, *The Coming of the French Revolution*, pp. 41–45.

25. See Rabb, *The Struggle for Stability in Early Modern Europe*, pp. 89–90.

26. Cf. Fox-Genovese and Genovese, *Fruits of Merchant Capital*, pp. 7–15; Anderson, *Lineages*, pp. 40–42.

27. Marx, "Moralising Criticism and Critical Morality," *CW* 6:328.

28. See Marx's review of Guizot's pamphlet, "Pourquoi la révolution d'Angleterre a-t-elle réussi? Discours sur l'histoire de la révolution d'Angleterre," *CW* 10:253–54. See also Hill, *The Century of Revolution*, pp. 24–27; Kemp, p. 37.

29. Marx, "Moralising Criticism and Critical Morality," *CW* 6:333.

30. Marx, *The German Ideology*, *CW* 5:90.

31. Ibid., pp. 68–72. Cf. Marx, *Grundrisse*, pp. 510–11.

32. Marx, Letter to Annenkov, 28 December 1846, *CW* 38:97.

33. Marx, *Capital* 3:332.

34. Ibid., p. 327.

35. A. B. Hibbert, "The Economic Policies of Towns," in *Economic Organization and Policies in the Middle Ages*, Vol. 3 of *The Cambridge Economic History of Europe*, eds. M. M. Postan, E. E. Rich and Edward Miller (Cambridge: Cambridge Univ. Press, 1963), p. 160.

36. Marx, *Capital* 3:325–26. See also Kriedte, *Peasants, Landlords and Merchant Capitalists. 1500–1800*, pp. 9, 40, 90, 131.

37. Hibbert, "The Economic Policies of Towns," pp. 158–59, 161–62.

38. Marx, *Capital* 3:329.

39. Ibid., p. 328.

40. Ibid., p. 330.

41. This and the following paragraph draw mainly upon Hibbert, "The Economic Policies of Towns," pp. 162–68.

42. Marx, *Capital* 3:330–31. Cf. John Merrington, "Town and Country in the Transition to Capitalism," in *The Transition From Feudalism to Capitalism*, ed. R. Hilton, p. 181.

43. Hibbert, "The Origins of the Medieval Town Patriciate," pp. 18–23, and "The Economic Policies of Towns," pp. 198–99.

44. Marx, *Capital* 3:335.

45. Ibid., p. 330.

46. Ibid., pp. 325–26.

47. Ibid., pp. 327, 332.

48. In his later works, Marx emphatically rejected the equation of capitalism with commercial relations and money markets, chastising Weber's mentor, Mommsen, for example, precisely for discovering "a capitalist mode of production in every monetary economy. . . . " *Capital* 3:787.

49. Marx, *Capital* 3:328.

50. Marx, *Capital* 1:167.

51. Marx, *Capital* 3:328. Cf. Brenner, "The Origins of Capitalist Development," pp. 49–51.

52. Marx, *Capital* 3:331–332.

53. Ibid., pp. 325–326. See also Kriedte, pp. 7–8.

54. Hilton, "A Comment," p. 116. See also Hibbert, "The Origins of the Medieval Town Patriciate," p. 17; Braudel, *The Structures of Everyday Life*, p. 510.

55. Merrington, "Town and Country in the Transition to Capitalism," p. 180.

56. Rodney Hilton, "Warriors and Peasants," p. 93. See also Hilton, "Feudalism in Europe: Problems for Historical Materialists," pp. 91–92.

57. Brenner, "The Origins of Capitalist Development," pp. 46, 60, 71.

58. It is true that to the extent that the lords' exactions took the form of money rents, the peasants were compelled to put more of their surplus up for sale. Although the peasants' need for money tied them more closely to the market, the transfer of their surplus to the lords meant that it was still largely the lords, not the peasants, who determined the character of effective demand.

59. Kemp, p. 70.

60. See Kemp, p. 70; Kriedte, p. 116; Barry Supple, "The Nature of Enterprise," in *The Economic Organization of Early Modern Europe, The Cambridge Economic History of Europe*, ed. E. E. Rich and C. H. Wilson 5:429–32.

61. Marx, *Capital* 3:334–35. The following discussion draws upon:

Merrington, "Town and Country in the Transition to Capitalism," pp. 177–80; Goubert, *The Ancien Regime*, pp. 205–08; Takahashi, "A Contribution to the Discussion," pp. 87–97; Hilton, "Feudalism in Europe," pp. 90–91; Unwin, Chs. 2 and 3. Unwin's works, like good wine, seem to improve with age: they "still provide us," writes Hilton, "with [some] of the best theoretically oriented analyses in English of craft production." "Introduction," to *The Transition From Feudalism to Capitalism*, p. 20, n. 11.

62. Marx, *Capital* 1:339. See also Kriedte, pp. 7–8.

63. Kriedte, p. 10.

64. Ibid., p. 40.

65. See Clark and Slack eds., *English Towns in Transition, 1500–1700*, pp. 106–07.

66. Rodney Hilton, "Medieval Market Towns and Simple Commodity Production," p. 4. Kriedte, p. 90.

67. Marx, *Capital* 3:334–35.

68. Brenner, "The Origins of Capitalist Development," p. 47.

69. E. J. Hobsbawm, "The Crisis of the Seventeenth Century," now reprinted with other contributions to the debate in *Crisis in Europe, 1560–1660*, ed. Trevor Aston, pp. 5–58. See also the contributions to *The General Crisis of the Seventeenth Century*, ed. Parker and Smith. Rabb offers an exhaustive review of the literature: see *The Struggle for Stability in Early Modern Europe*, pp. 3–34. Kriedte provides an invaluable survey of the crisis: see *Peasants, Landlords and Merchant Capitalists*, pp. 61–100.

70. See in particular Ivo Schoffer, "Did Holland's Golden Age Coincide with a Period of Crisis?" in *The General Crisis of the Seventeenth Century*, ed. Parker and Smith, pp. 87, 104–05; Lublinskaya, *French Absolutism: The Crucial Phase, 1620–1629*, pp. 41–43. Cf. Pierre Goubert, "Local History," pp. 306–08.

71. Rabb, p. 83.

72. Ibid., pp. 85, 87. See also Kriedte, pp. 61–70.

73. Hobsbawm, "The Crisis of the Seventeenth Century," in *Crisis in Europe, 1560–1660*, ed. Trevor Aston, p. 5–6.

74. Hobsbawm, to be sure, is well aware that merchant's capital could prove overwhelmingly conservative. Capital investment, he argued, was blind: whether it was led to revolutionize production or drawn toward an accommodation with the old order depended upon the existing opportunities for realizing the maximum profit. Ibid., pp. 15–16. Nevertheless, he maintained that the seventeenth century crisis dealt a mortal blow to merchant capital's parasitic attachment to the feudal economy, simultaneously foreclosing this avenue of obtain-

ing a surplus and opening certain promising opportunities for capitalist enterprise. Hobsbawm, however, never specifies the internal dynamic of the crisis whereby these ends were accomplished. One is left with the distinct impression that, in the course of the crisis, society's institutional framework was somehow forcibly adapted to the requirements of economic progress. Ibid., p. 27. Rabb has found this conclusion particularly objectionable (see pp. 87–88), and on this score he is correct. Cf. Lublinskaya, pp. 43–75.

75. Anderson, *Lineages*, p. 18. Cf. Rabb, pp. 64–65, 96, 98, 118.

76. Anderson, *Lineages*, pp. 52–55; Rabb, pp. 60–73.

77. Anderson, *Lineages*, pp. 19–20. This paragraph is based, in large part, on Anderson's excellent discussion of the internal structure of the absolutist state: see Ibid., 29–40. See also Kriedte, pp. 98–99.

78. Anderson, p. 18.

79. It also had alternative outcomes in diverse social formations: only in England did it precipitate feudalism's final collapse, leading to the emergence of social conditions that permitted an unprecedented triumph of capitalism.

80. Rabb, pp. 88–89; Kriedte. pp. 70–74.

81. Nield Steensgaard,"The Seventeenth Century Crisis," in *The General Crisis of the Seventeenth Century*, pp. 29–36; Rabb, 85–87.

82. This is the question posed by Schoffer, referring to the reluctance of Dutch historians to assent to the characterization of the seventeenth century—Holand's "golden age"—as a period of crisis. "Did Holland's Golden Age Coincide with a Period of Crisis?" in *The General Crisis of the Seventeenth Century*, ed. Parker and Smith, p. 87. Cf. Wallerstein, *The Modern World System* 2:13–26.

83. Referring to textile production, the most important medieval industry, Steensgaard argues that French manufacture changed over to luxury production from around 1660 onwards. The northern Netherlands began to produce more expensive goods in the early decades of the century; the southern Netherlands around mid-century. "The Seventeenth Century Crisis," pp. 32–33.

84. See Steensgaard, "The Seventeenth Century Crisis," pp. 39, 40–41; Hobsbawm, "The Crisis of the Seventeenth Century," in *Crisis in Europe, 1560–1660*, ed. Trevor Aston, pp. 19, 26, 47.

85. Anderson, *Lineages* p. 40.

86. See Kriedte, pp. 72 (fig. 14), 76, 79–87; Brenner, "Agrarian Class Structure and Economic Development," pp. 52–55.

87. See Merrington, "Town and Country in the Transition to Capitalism," pp. 183–88.

88. Carlo M. Cipolla, *Before the Industrial Revolution*, 2nd ed. (New York: W. W. Norton, 1980), pp. 253–63; Hobsbawm, "The Crisis of the Seventeenth Century," pp. 18–20.

89. Hobsbawm, "The Crisis of the Seventeenth Century," pp. 41–43; Schoffer, "Holland's Golden Age," pp. 97–100; Wallerstein, *The Modern World System*, 2:70; Kriedte, pp. 76–77, 87–88, 90–91. The production of the most important Dutch textile center, Leiden, increased during the early part of the century only by "concentrating to an increasing extent on the production of more expensive goods; the production of the cheaper new draperies began to decline as early as the 1620s." Steensgaard, "The Seventeenth Century Crisis," p. 32. See also Kriedte, pp. 76–77. A good indicator showing that seventeenth century Dutch growth remained trapped within a Continent-wide feudal framework is the fate of its rural economy. Although Holland's agriculture achieved remarkable progress at this time, it was essentially bound to the Continental cycle of population growth—ecological imbalance—demographic exhaustion. See Wilson, "The Historical Study of Economic Growth and Decline in Early Modern Europe," 25–26; E. L. Jones, "Editor's Introduction," p. 21; Rabb, p. 86; Brenner, "The Agrarian Roots of European Capitalism," pp. 325–26.

90. Anderson, *Lineages*, p. 103; Steensgaard, "The Seventeenth Century Crisis," p. 33; Kemp, pp. 73–76.

91. Le Roy Ladurie, *The Peasants of Languedoc*, pp. 219ff., 234–238, 292–96.

92. See Kriedte, p. 77.

93. Taylor, "Non-Capitalist Wealth and the Origins of the French Revolution," pp. 469–96, and "Types of Capitalism in Eighteenth Century France," pp. 478–97. Taylor develops this concept to explain French developments, but it clearly has wider applications to the late feudal regime as a whole. On the response of Dutch merchants, see Kriedte, pp. 76, 90–91, 99.

94. Merrington, "Town and Country in the Transition to Capitalism," p. 184. See also Bloch, *French Rural History*, pp. 124ff.; Goubert, *The Ancien Regime*, pp. 241–42; Rabb, p. 96; Kriedte, pp. 92, 97.

95. Anderson, *Lineages*, p. 97.

96. Brenner, "Agrarian Class Structure and Economic Development," pp. 51–52, and "The Origins of Capitalist Development," pp. 72–73; Parker and Smith, pp. 8–9, 10–12; Steensgaard, "The Seventeenth Century Crisis," pp. 28–31, 41; Hobsbawm, "The Crisis of the Seventeenth Century," pp. 6–14; Wallerstein, *The Modern World System*, 2:14; Goubert, *The Ancien Regime*, pp. 36–42; Kriedte, pp. 63, 65–

66, 91–94. This is also true of Holland, in the midst of its "Golden Age."

97. Anderson, *Lineages*, pp. 32–33; Rabb, pp. 60–63; Kriedte, pp. 92–93. It appears that exorbitant taxes were in some measure responsible for depleting agricultural resources and impairing rural growth in the Dutch Republic as well: "the Republic, from a population half as large as that of England and one-sixth of that of France, extracted a public revenue larger than that of England and a third of that raised by France." Wilson, "The Historical Study of Economic Growth and Decline in Early Modern History," p. 25.

98. Brenner, "The Origins of Capitalist Development," p. 73; Steensgaard, "The Seventeenth Century Crisis," pp. 36–42.

99. Kriedte, p. 98.

100. Rabb, pp. 64–65, 94–96, 118–19.

101. *Capital* 3:334.

102. Hilton, "Medieval Market Towns," p. 22.

103. Kriedte, pp. 90–91.

104. *Capital* 3:333.

105. See Hill, *Reformation to Industrial Revolution*, pp. 245–46; Goubert, *The Ancien Regime*, pp. 220–21; Clarkson, p. 231; Hobsbawm, *Industry and Empire*, pp. 59–65. The issue of the relationship between ways number one and number two was a central point of contention in the debate on the transition to capitalism occasioned by Dobb's *Studies in the Development of Capitalism*. See Hilton, ed., *The Transition From Feudalism to Capitalism*.

106. See Marx, *Capital* 1:339; Kriedte, p. 12; Unwin, Chs. 5 and 6.

107. Hibbert, "The Economic Policies of Towns," p. 204. See also Hilton, "Introduction," pp. 21–22, and "Capitalism—What's in a Name?" pp. 151–52; Braudel, *The Wheels of Commerce*, pp. 317–20.

108. Hill, *Reformation to Industrial Revolution*, pp. 90–92, 169–70; Clark and Slack, *English Towns in Transition*, pp. 35–45. Robert Darnton provides a good account of the process of economic differentiation between masters and workers in the printing shops of mid-eighteenth century France in *The Great Cat Massacre and Other Episodes in French Cultural History*, pp. 78–82.

109. Thompson, *The Making of the English Working Class*, pp. 269–90.

110. Ibid., pp. 221–22.

111. Marx, *Capital* 1:478.

112. Marx, *Capital* 3:785–86.

5

From Feudalism to Capitalism: The Transformation of the Countryside

Capitalism is a historically circumscribed mode of exploitation distinguished by the specific form in which surplus labor is extracted from the direct producers. The accumulation of wealth as *capital* therefore presupposes the prior establishment of capitalist class relations.[1] Accordingly, Marx's account of the genesis of capitalism is essentially an account of the process which created a capitalist class, owning the means of production, facing a working class, owning nothing but labor power.[2] This process, he argues, was marked by two decisive events. The first comprised the abolition of all types of personal dependence—that is, of serfdom. The ordinary producers thereby obtained the right to deploy their labor power and its product as they wished. The emancipation of labor fulfilled an essential prerequisite of capitalist exploitation: If the individual is to sell his labor power as a commodity, explains Marx, "he must have it at his disposal, must be the untrammelled owner of his capacity for labour, i.e., of his person."[3] Yet clearly this condition alone did not suffice to create a labor market: Since the direct producers retained control over productive resources on which they could get a living by their work, the only necessary exchange of commodities was between the products of labor, not labor power itself. Consequently, the second essential prerequisite of capitalist accumulation is that "the labourer, instead of being in the position to sell commodities in which his labour is incorporated, must be obliged to offer for sale as a commodity that very labour-power, which exists only in his living self."[4] The fulfillment of this condition entailed the forcible expropriation of the more or less independent peasantry from the soil, stripping them of every productive resource except their labor power. Expropriation was achieved primarily by acts of enclosure, which created compact farms individually owned as exclusive property.[5] Enclosure—"a plain enough case of class robbery," wrote E. P. Thompson—transformed the peasant cultivators' customary relations to the agrarian means of production, terminating the panoply of common rights which protected them from utter proletarianization.

Our examination of Marx's historical writings on feudalism and merchant capitalism ruled out—contrary to some of his more general theoretical pronouncements—two explanations of the formation of capitalist class relations. First, the course of development of feudal class struggle did not nurture within itself a class with the capacity and the interest to revolutionize the society as a whole. The peasants irreparably impaired the lords' capacity to live as lords. But this struggle proved quite inadequate to raise the peasantry to a position of dominance. Needless to say, a capitalist class emerged from the process of disintegration of feudal society. But this class was not called into existence by feudalism's inherent dynamic; nor did its ascendance occasion feudalism's collapse. Second, the transition to capitalism cannot be understood in terms of the emergence of a set of vigorous productive forces which, at a given point, precipitated a realignment of the increasingly obsolete property system in a manner designed to permit continued economic growth. No amount of wealth, extent of long-distance trade or level of technological development can account for the accumulation of capital. On the contrary, it is the existence of capitalist class relations which, once in place, determines the form wealth takes and the extent to which technically and organizationally useful knowledge is converted into forces of production.

Marx refers the question of the advent of capitalism to the question of the processes of class struggle, which gave rise to it. A study of Marx's answer shows that the two essential prerequisites of capitalist production—the emancipation of the direct producers, and their expropriation from the means of production—were fulfilled on either side of the transition between feudalism and capitalism. They comprised different stages in the historical trajectories of two distinct class systems—one waning, the other ascending. Accordingly, each of these twin preconditions was established by qualitatively different types of class conflict. The first was the result of the struggle within the feudal mode of production; the second required a struggle between the declining feudal and the rising capitalist modes of production.

This chapter is divided into three sections. The first argues that feudal class relations unravelled from within: Successful peasant struggle irreversibly loosened the grip of aristocratic domination, releasing in the process a class of ordinary producers enjoying an unprecedented economic autonomy. The class struggle within feudalism, however, was incapable by itself of generating a capitalist alternative: the outcome of the conflict between lords and peasants culminated not in the revolutionary reconstitution of society at large, but in the common ruin of the contending classes.[6]

The second section argues that only an advanced *prior* disintegration of the feudal mode of exploitation "set free the elements" that made necessary and possible the organization of the capitalist mode of exploitation.[7] The consolidation of the new economic order, however, required the ascending class to complete the destruction of the traditional regime. Clearly, if capitalist private property was to do the whole task of allocating labor power and its product, then all productive resources, including labor power, had to be compelled to assume the new property form. Accordingly, the transfer of power from one ruling class to another manifested itself in the clash between incompatible class systems: the existing regime sought to preserve and restore its institutional foundations, and the ascendant class to replace them with the conditions necessary for its rule.

The success of the nascent capitalist class in disentangling itself from the remnants of the inherited order gave rise to the historically new mode of production. The bourgeois revolutions sorted out the struggles within and between class systems. This process is examined in the third section, a study of the English and French Revolutions.

Marx cautioned that his analysis of the genesis of capitalism was confined to Western Europe and, more specifically, to England.[8] Accordingly, we shall study his conception of the transition from feudalism to capitalism by comparing the outcomes of class struggle in the English and French countryside between the fifteenth and the eighteenth centuries. This contrast will illuminate the conditions under which the consolidation of capitalist relations of production became a historical possibility.

AGRARIAN RELATIONS IN ENGLAND AND FRANCE, 1450–1750

The Abolition of Serfdom: England

The general crisis of the fourteenth century unleashed a desperate class struggle on the land that proved to be the turning point in the dissolution of dependent cultivation in Western Europe. This process developed earliest and furthest in England, where successful peasant resistance irreparably crippled the lords' capacity to continue to live as lords—that is, to wield jurisdictional authority over the persons and properties of their tenants. The nexus of sovereignty and property that constituted the true differentia of the institution of landlordship began to wither away.

In the context of the acute labor shortage created by the general crisis, the peasants brought labor services to an end, forcing the lords to wind up their demesnes in a radical and permanent manner.[9] Throughout the fifteenth century, these lands were let out piecemeal to smaller tenants, mostly villagers, or whole to the community of villagers, who divided it amongst themselves, or (less commonly) to single individuals or a group of partners, usually wealthier peasants. The demesne thus came to lose its traditional and customary role in the lord's manor: it was typically broken up and its land passed over to be used according to the interests of the producers.

The other side of the collapse of demesne cultivation was the peasants' remarkable achievement in ameliorating or emancipating their economic conditions of life from the jurisdictional and administrative authority of the manor.[10] The direct producers irreparably destroyed their dependent position, wresting from the lords the right to dispose of their persons and their properties as they wished. There was no question of a reimposition of individual legal serfdom after the fifteenth century. Peasant families gained the freedom to move in search of higher wages or better holdings at improved terms of tenure, or to marry off single women outside the manor; to devote most of their labor and its product to the cultivation and maintenance of the holding; to conclude agreements regarding the disposition of their properties, principally to buy, sell or let land; to bequeath an inheritance and to inherit property. Moreover, they unburdened themselves from a panoply of economic disabilities that accompanied servile villeinage: amercements, or fines levied by the manorial court for a whole range of offences against the lord's rights; chevage or recognitions; tallage, the manorial tax, and so on.

The economic emancipation of the peasantry found expression in profound changes overtaking the nature and terms of land tenure—away from customary, and toward free forms of land holding.[11]

> In England, serfdom had practically disappeared in the last part of the 14th century. The immense majority of the population consisted then, and to a still larger extent, in the 15th century, of free peasant proprietors, whatever was the feudal title under which their right of property was hidden.[12]

The traditional and customary terms of tenure governing the relationship between landlord and subjects were slowly transformed into "purely money relationships fixed contractually in accordance with the rules of positive law."[13] But there were still significant differences in the feudal titles under which the new forms of peasant tenure were hidden, differences which carried important consequences for the evolution of English agriculture. First, increasing amounts of land were transformed into peasant freehold: the cultivator bought or rented land on free terms or liquidated his rent obligation to the lord, to all intents and purposes becoming "an independent peasant with complete ownership of the land he tills."[14] Second, substantial tracts of land were turned into leasehold: here, "the possessor engaged in agriculture becomes virtually a mere tenant."[15] And lastly, customary tenure lost its association with servility and became copyhold. Probably the most widespread form of tenure, copyhold combined features of freehold and leasehold.

There had, of course, always been land which had escaped feudal subjection in medieval Europe, and England was no exception. Free terms could also be proffered by the lord as an incentive to recruit settlers, or bought by wealthier peasants. These freeholds were typically inheritable and could be enforced in the public courts. Free tenants had the right to dispose of their own person and property and, if they did not own their lands outright, their rents were considerably lower than those levied on customary tenants. In effect, freeholders were owner-occupiers. Their share of the land increased following the fourteenth century crisis, as financial embarrassment forced both the Crown and the lords to sell land. The sale of charters of manumission to peasants seeking free status and tenure was one of the last profits lords extracted from serfdom. It is also likely that, given the acute shortage of tenants, lords made considerable concessions to interest new ones in occupying vacant holdings. It is from the ranks of the freeholders, together with tenants possessing inheritable copyholds and even the lesser gentry, that the class of English yeomen was recruited.

Equally significant, late medieval England witnessed an evolution of peasant tenures towards leasehold, typically limited to a term of years and subject to a purely economic rent normally paid in money. In this way, substantial amounts of land were withdrawn from the jurisdiction of custom altogether. The principal sources of land let on noncustomary terms were the lords' demesnes which, we have seen, were being wound down in the late fourteenth and fifteenth centuries, or lapsed tenements which remained under the lords' control. Freeholders and copyholders themselves contributed to the growth of leaseholds by engaging in short-term subletting amongst themselves.

The significance of the development of leasehold, clearly, is that it extricated land from the tangle of customary rules, releasing it to be used at the discretion of the individual: leaseholds "were almost invariably for terms of years so that the rent and other conditions of tenure could be adjusted according to market conditions at the end of the term."[16]

The majority of holdings in late medieval England, however, were still held on customary terms, the most important of which was copyhold. Copyhold was a form of customary tenure which, without being legally enfranchised, was unencumbered by the burdens of servility. It was typically held not only by free peasants, but by lesser gentry as well, who acquired portions of copyhold land to round off their estates. The shift to copyhold was widespread by the beginning of the fifteenth century; by the middle of this century common law was hesitantly beginning to protect its security. Its terms of tenure were determined by manorial custom and recorded on the rolls of the manor court, a copy of which was issued to the tenant. The possession of a deed often gave occupiers the idea that a contract had been concluded between free individuals. Indeed, in the atmosphere of peasant self-assertiveness, many copyholds were practically free: they carried rights of inheritance, their annual rents and the appurtenances and fines associated with them were fixed, and they were freely negotiable. However, since their conditions of tenure were determined by manorial custom, copyholds varied enormously, usually in accordance with the relative strength of lord and peasant from estate to estate, even from manor to manor. Copyholds were commonly held for life (averaging twenty years) or lives (usually three), subject to variable entry fines. Most significantly, copyhold never succeeded in acquiring the security of tenure enforceable at common law equivalent to freehold, and the variable entry fines permitted adjustments in the terms of tenure according to economic conditions. This situation was not inimical to peasant interests in the fifteenth century. However, it proved to be the weak point in manorial custom: when the balance of class forces swung decisively against them, it would permit the dispossession of the cultivators from their lands.

The story of the way in which peasant tenures lost the disabilities of servility and acquired the advantages associated with freehold was only one side of the improvement in the economic situation of the direct producers. The other was the growing size of their holdings. Lapsed or empty tenements, left vacant by the Black Death, or land let by the Crown and by the lords, allowed most peasants to obtain a small plot if they possessed none, a larger one if they did. The fifteenth century English village did not witness a process of marked differentiation within the ranks of the agricultural producers, creating a class of wealthy "kulaks" at one pole and landless laborers at the other. Their internal economic divisions would become accentuated only later, after the decay of the manorial regime had allowed the village economy to mature, loosening its cohesion. In the immediate aftermath of the crisis, however, "economic promotion" rather than "economic differentiation" would better describe developments within the peasant community.[17] If the emergence of a wealthier peasant yeomanry is unmistakable, so is the improvement in the economic condition of all ranks of villagers. The largest holdings became larger, but the smallest holdings and the landless fewer. "Only in the period of the decline and fall of the feudal system," wrote Marx, "but where it still struggles internally—as in England in the fourteenth and first half of the fifteenth centuries—is there a golden age for labor in the process of becoming emancipated."[18] The majority of English peasant families obtained land on which they could get a living by their labor; there was probably a decline in the number of families who depended on regular employment for wages compared with other sections of the population.[19]

The Petty Mode of Production: A Nursery School for Capitalist Tenants

The emancipation of the English peasantry loosened the economic base of the feudal mode of production, the village community, from the shackles of lordship, allowing it to develop according to its own inherent propensities.[20] The peasantry retained effective control over the organization of production. Feudal restrictions on peasant agriculture collapsed, and the lords made little attempt at this time to determine husbandry practices by their leasing policies. The autonomy of the small producers permitted them to create a relatively unfettered economy of petty commodity production. It is within this economy, Marx suggests, that the prelude to the history of capitalist accumulation was played. Its internal dynamic brought forth the material agencies which simultaneously destroyed the cohesion of the peasantry as a class, making possible their eventual expropriation from the land, and created the basis for a revolution in agricultural production.[21]

The dissolution of feudal rule occasioned the dissolution of the concrete foundation of collective peasant resistance, the village community, as a coherent organism.[22] The peasants' talent for organization and concerted action, we have seen, was rooted in the necessity to tightly regulate economic activity imposed by the practice of farming in open or common fields. Each individual peasant family did not independently determine the disposition of its labor power and resources within the rural economy. The agricultural system required the close collaboration of all villagers to ensure the proper distribution of tasks necessary to reproduce the material life of the whole community. The village was not, of course, an idyl of cooperation. Economic conflict, particularly between rich and poor, was common. The poor were normally required to work for, rent, or borrow from the wealthy in order to ensure their livelihood. Moreover, it was the village notables who typically controlled the administration of local affairs. These divisions became progressively more accentuated with economic development, giving rise to increasingly frequent clashes over terms of access to the arable and the commons, and over rents and wages.

The conflict within the village, however, had always been sharply circumscribed by the conflict between the village and the lords. "Their antagonism," writes Rodney Hilton, "could be compared rather to a family quarrel than to the hostility arising from a social gulf."[23] First, the internal stratification of the peasant economy was limited by the lords' demands on its surplus, which prevented the scale of production from growing beyond the point where a holding would require a substantial supply of labor to work it.[24] Second, contention was always checked by the need to protect common interests against the claims of the nobility. Compared with the deep horizontal cleavage between lord and peasant, the antagonism within peasant society could indeed be referred to as a conflict within a family: in fact, the "children of the household were often classified as servants within the household."[25] The community of villagers showed a remarkable degree of solidarity and self-consciousness in repelling landlord encroachments upon their economic conditions of existence.

These conditions of peasant cohesiveness were destroyed by the very success of the class struggle against feudal exploitation they made possible.[26] The emancipation of the petty mode of production simultaneously permitted peasant agriculture to attain the highest development of which it was capable and spelled the end of village solidarity. Unencumbered by the harsh constraints of the manorial regime, the peasants were able to introduce a greater degree of economic rationality into their agricultural practices. The freedom to dispose of their lands and labor gave peasants the requisite flexibility to increase their revenues by taking advantage of the growing market. The disruptive impact of the lords' demands was at a minimum. Yet, at the same time, the increasing mobility of the peasant population and the multiplying number of land sales and leases tended to disperse the communities of arable farmers, breaking up the ancient tenemental arrangements that had given peasant villages their internal solidity and resilience.

More significantly, the peasants were able to retain increasing amounts of surplus within the household economy, allowing them to invest profits to improve production. Manorial and royal exactions had dropped precipitously. The vital element in this development was the yeomanry, a group comprised mainly of substantial freeholders and copyholders, shading off toward poorer husbandmen below and lesser gentry above them. They had both sufficient resources and the will to break away from the inherited agricultural routine and introduce new methods of working the land. They experimented with agricultural techniques, crops, land management, and brought new terrain under cultivation.

These changes in the conduct of agriculture required the enclosing and engrossing of holdings. Both spelled the end of the open fields. The peasants did not have a generalized attachment to the village community. When they saw the concrete possibility of improving their economic situation by reorganizing their farms, they took it. The well-to-do cultivators especially were released from the imperative to preserve village unity to press the struggle against the lords, once the manorial economy was wrecked beyond repair. "Rich peasant families," writes Hilton, "now graziers and demesne farmers holding largely by leasehold tenure, no longer stood as mediators between the lords and the communities of customary tenants. They were no longer potential leaders in the resistance."[27]

It is clear tht the yeomen were the initial force behind the enclosures: They amalgamated scattered land parcels by appropriating, very often illegally, lapsed holdings, by nibbling away at wastes, commons and not infrequently neighboring fields, including those of inattentive lords. Much enclosure was accomplished in the form of mutual "agreements" between the substantial freeholders of the village to consolidate plots. "It is difficult to avoid the impression," Christopher Hill comments, "that on occasion 'agreement' was extorted from the weak by the strong."[28] If, then, the petty mode of production was a result of the "economic promotion" of the ordinary producers, its further evolution resulted in a progressive "economic differentiation" within their ranks. The collaboration which had characterized the agricultural system broke down, overwhelmed by their increasingly disparate interests. The wealthy yeomen began to thrust upward, adopting the concerns of the gentry rather than those of subsistence cultivators. "They went to the same schools, came to share their outlook, and were prepared to follow their lead."[29]

The emergence of the economy of free-peasant proprietorship within the framework of a collapsing manorial regime, Marx argues, was the decisive development in the formation and breakthrough of capitalist class relations. The process of good husbandry and painstaking accumulation of capital in land, often in the form of small savings, gave rise to a marked improvement in rural productivity, ultimately culminating in a revolution in agricultural production.[30] The well-to-do peasants, Marx writes,

> gradually acquire the possibility of accumulating a certain amount of wealth and themselves [become] transformed into future capitalists. The old self-employed possessors of land themselves thus give rise to a nursery school for capitalist tenants, whose development is conditioned by the general development of capitalist production beyond the bounds of the country-side. This class shoots up very rapidly when particularly favourable circumstances come to its aid, as in England in the 16th century, where the then progressive depreciation of money enriched them under the customary long leases at the expense of the landlords.[31]

But if the petty mode of production provided the nursery school for capitalist farming, it was also the death bed of the peasantry as a class. *Both* occurrences, we shall see, were required for the rise of the capitalist mode of production. The peasants showed the lords the profits that adoption of new farming methods could bring. Concomitantly, the peasants' loss of solidarity made it possible for the lords to develop these methods on a larger scale by facilitating the evacuation of the cultivators from their holdings.[32] This argument will be developed below. Presently, we turn to examine the composition of the rural economy of the ancien regime in France. This comparative study will allow a more precise evaluation of the nature of the peasantry's contribution to the transition to capitalism.

The Survival of Feudalism: France

In contrast to England, the French peasant community remained enmeshed in the seigneurial net down to the final suppression of the ancien regime by the Revolution of 1789. It is clear that this is the principal feature distinguishing the agrarian structures of the two countries at the close of the Middle Ages. In England, the general crisis of European feudalism definitively ruptured the nexus linking lord and peasant. English lords were unable to stem the drainage of the powers of lordship, producing the weakest and shortest royal absolutism; when the country landowners reasserted their collective power, it was no longer by means of the manorial court, but in sessions of the peace. At the same time, as we have seen, customary tenure in England gave the ordinary cultivators a precarious hold on their lands, permitting their expropriation at a later date. In France, by contrast, the nobility reconstituted the feudal apparatus whereby it coerced a surplus from the rural economy by regrouping itself around the most formidable absolute monarchy in Western Europe.[33] Seigneurial justice retained its "economic" powers, but relinquished most of its "political" ones to the crown:

> On top of the direct levy, an excess levy in taxation was imposed permanently, the major portion of which flowed by numerous channels into seigneurial treasuries. There was nothing revolutionary in this. The two basic classes of society remained face to face. . . . The power of the prince henceforth protected that of the lord, extracting from peasant production whatever was needed to maintain the ruling class.[34]

Concomitantly, the village community succeeded in wresting for its cultivators the *hereditary* usufruct of their holdings. Petty peasant proprietorship thereby consolidated its hold on the countryside.

Although the power of the lords to command an income had fallen steeply in the immediate aftermath of the crisis, seigneurial claims on the peasants were far from worthless. Many had simply fallen into desuetude. If, then, this process could be put in reverse, a stricter, rationalized exploitation of the seigneurie would recoup lost revenues. These innovations were pioneered by the new lords of recent bourgeois extraction, schooled in the business practices of the cities. The old nobility had been seriously debilitated by the general crisis; by 1500, when the downward trend of estate revenues had passed its nadir, many houses of ancient lineage had been ruined. When it began in the sixteenth century, reconstruction was fueled in large measure by urban capital. Its penetration into the countryside, however, did not fundamentally alter class relations on the land. Quite the contrary, the most stubbornly cherished ideal of the bourgeoisie was to cap commercial success with nobility, and one of the principal paths to ennoblement was through the purchase of seigneuries.[35] Patrician families had of course always sought safe investment havens in the land. The sixteenth century, however, witnessed the single largest influx of urban capital into the countryside. "This advance by the bourgeoisie," wrote Marc Bloch, " . . . was the most decisive event in French social history, especially in its rural aspect."[36] Its principal effect was to revive the whole seigneurial structure.

This "rent offensive" wove the seigneurie into the fabric of the ancien regime, imprinting its essential character. The new landlords adopted more efficient means of collecting agricultural revenues; they revived ancient claims that had not been pressed or pressed too lightly; generalized burdens throughout a region, imposing obligations customary in one village upon a neighboring one which had so far escaped them; deduced hitherto unnoticed economic implications of existing disabilities; and discovered wholly new charges in the tangle of rules governing the relationship between landlord and tenant.

This economic pressure weighed heavily on the countryside: the cultivators once again found themselves subject to oppressive claims on their labor and its product.[37] To be sure, the majority were now personally free. The lord's claim to a revenue was a function of superior rights in the land, which precluded the cultivator who "held" it from disposing of it or its product without first securing the lord's permission, typically by purchasing it. On the whole, the panoply of feudal disabilities raked off no less than one-fifth, often reaching twice and sometimes three times that amount, of the "gross" yield of peasant production. The actual share levied by the feudal ruling class, of course, varied widely across regions and time depending on the relative strengths of lords and peasants. Still, rental claims were oppressive enough in normal times; in times of crisis, they pushed vast numbers of peasants into beggary, vagrancy, and death.

The French peasants did not, however, confront these inroads upon their conditions of life merely as an inert aggregate. Quite the contrary, the very seigneurial offensive reanimated the village community, the locus of peasant class struggle: It was precisely the necessity of protecting their interests against the hostile interests of their common enemy, the lords, that compelled the peasants (despite their internal divisions and tensions) to maintain their solidarity and self-consciousness. Village life was organized around the *terroir*:

> The sum of all types of land cultivated or exploited by a group of men either centered on a big village or around several hamlets or else dispersed over a patchwork of scattered holdings. The unity of the *terroir* is always sanctioned and embodied by a communal body, the 'assembly of inhabitants', which abides by traditional rulings and occasionally makes new ones to ensure that where the exploitation of land is the concern of the community it operates in the common interest.[38]

Two late-medieval developments strengthened the capacity of the peasant villages to resist seigneurial pressure. First, as we have seen, French cultivators held their lands by inheritance.[39] The reemergence of Roman law during the later Middle Ages prompted juristic efforts to simplify the tangle of customary rules governing land use. One of their fruits was the notion of "seisin," "an intermediate conception between Latin 'property' and 'possession', which guaranteed a protected ownership against casual appropriations and conflicting claims, while retaining the feudal principle of multiple titles to the same object."[40] In time this idea hardened, giving the cultivators hereditary rights to their holdings. By the sixteenth century, the inheritance of tenures was incontestable; by the eighteenth, the peasant village was deeply entrenched in the land.

The second development strengthening the hand of the village community was the steady migration of the landlords away from the countryside to the town, preferably the capital.[41] The seigneur was rarely present on his estates, his relation to the land narrowing to a purely parasitic one—receipt of the mixture of rents owed him. The seigneurie no longer played a military role and its law-enforcement functions in the *terroir* "had been taken over by the peasant magistracies, with the supervision and occasional assistance of the intendants and their subordinates."[42] As a result, the peasant community was free to develop a substantial degree of self-government. To be sure, as in the past, the management of local affairs was informally controlled by a small minority of wealthy cultivators. Still, the communal life of the peasants provided the material basis and vital experiential context for articulating and organizing their common interests as a class.

The class struggle on the land determined the historical fate of the ancien regime:

> Ground rent—royal, seigneurial, tithe and proprietorial— [was] the driving force of the realm and of its social system. Rent payers were the ruled, receivers of rent and their agents the rulers. At least nine-tenths of the population of the realm [was] bracketed by this elementary contrast.[43]

The rent struggle impelled French economic development along a feudal path. The contrast with England is instructive.[44] We have seen that the English cultivators emancipated the petty mode of production from its feudal constraints. The village economy flourished, in time producing an entrepreneurial element, the yeomen, who shed their remaining disabilities and patiently accumulated capital in land, taking advantage of their autonomy to increase profits and reinvest them. The result was the beginning of a process of productive development which, by the seventeenth century, had advanced sufficiently to allow England to escape those massive demographic crises that periodically tore apart the social fabric on the Continent.

French lords, by contrast, succeeded in halting and then reversing the trend toward peasant emancipation evident in the immediate aftermath of the general crisis, tightening the meshes of the seigneurial net. The village economy, thus reintegrated within the feudal system, was given precious little room for development. The lords siphoned considerable amounts of surplus from peasant agriculture, returning little in the form of productive investments. Landlord demands in direct rents were surpassed by indirect state taxes, squeezing the peasant economy even further. Half of all royal revenues were consumed by warfare, the other half on maintaining the administrative apparatus and on magnificence and largess. The lords, for their part, typically adopted ways of life requiring levels of display which often drove them into debt and even bankruptcy—that is, "unless the king made a timely intervention, as he usually did."[45] The paucity of rural investment, writes Pierre Goubert, "expressed a lack of confidence in the land which remained a brake on the economic fate of the country for a long time."[46]

The most striking expression of the contrast between the agrarian economies of England and France in this period was the absence of any equivalent in the latter to the yeomanry. There were, to be sure, well-to-do peasants in all French villages, but they were a small minority. The vast majority led lives of complete dependence, with little chance for improvement; their lot was typically to sink rather than rise.[47] The results were fateful: the French economy was robbed of its most dynamic force—a truly independent peasantry. Population expansion in France thus repeatedly ran up against the ceiling on economic growth imposed by the ancien regime, producing demographic crises every thirty years or so until 1750.[48]

The alternative outcomes of the feudal class struggle in England and France determined the possibility for qualitative social transformation in the two social formations. In England, the peasantry's decisive triumph severed the feudal class relation, thus fulfilling the first prerequisite of the transition to capitalism—the emancipation of the direct producers from the institution of lordship. In France, by contrast, the reimposition of feudal rule ensured that the kingdom remained firmly "this side" of the great transformation for another one hundred and fifty years.

THE GENESIS OF CAPITALIST CLASS RELATIONS

The formation of the capitalist class entailed the fulfillment of the second prerequisite of the transition to capitalism—the expropriation of the cultivators from their holdings.

> The process . . . that clears the way for the capitalist system, can be none other than the process which takes away from the labourer the possession of his means of production; a process that transforms, on

> the one hand, the social means of subsistence and of production into capital, on the other, the immediate producers into wage-labourers. The so-called primitive accumulation, therefore, is nothing else than the historical process of divorcing the producer from the means of production.[49]

Clearly, the configuration of class relations which occasioned the collapse of feudalism was qualitatively different from that which governed the rise of capitalism. If the peasants were chiefly responsible for dismantling the old mode of exploitation, they were the main victims of the rise of the new. If the lords' capacity to live as lords withered away with the dissolution of the manorial regime, the rising class constituted itself in large part from enterprising elements among them, who undertook the reorganization of the agricultural system, completing the destruction of the old.

How can the transition from the dissolution of feudal class relations to the formation of capitalist class relations be explained? We can rule out the proposition that the landed upper classes adopted more efficient agricultural techniques in response to the profits they anticipated as a result of commercial expansion, particularly of overseas trade. This thesis is an extension of the argument that the transition to capitalism was impelled by the rise of merchant capitalism, in this case by its penetration into the countryside. In this view, the transformation of the agricultural system was a spontaneous adaptation of the rural elites to the growth of market demand: Urban based commodity production generated an economic pull which destabilized and undermined traditional rural relations. Rising prices induced the landowners to seek a better return from their lands by increasing production. The introduction of new methods of cultivation required in turn major changes in the composition of farms—that is, enclosing and engrossing. The culmination of this process was a qualitative change in the class system: Evicted from their holdings, the formerly independent cultivators were transformed into proletarians.

The main flaw in this argument is that it equates maximizing profits with maximizing productive development. They are not at all the same process; each is governed by entirely different principles. The appropriation of an economic surplus from the direct producers is determined by the class system, whereas technological progress is determined by the extent to which the surplus extracted is employed to improve the productive forces. Whether and to what degree the strategies individuals adopt to appropriate a surplus require them to make productive investments depends upon the nature of the class system. Thus, the mere presence of commercial opportunities did not determine the lords' economic activities. Throughout the Middle Ages, they had responded to the expansion of trade by attempting to *intensify* manorial pressure on the dependent population in order to increase the amount of surplus coming their way, which they then realized on the market. The lords did not, that is, apply the resources at their disposal to increase production, which indeed would have obliged them to alter the social structure of the countryside; they used their resources to augment surplus appropriation, that is, to reinforce the mechanisms of exploitation available to them.

This is the lesson of the contrasting methods of extracting an economic surplus used by English and French lords in the early modern epoch.[50] The pull of overseas demand was quite strong in both countries. Prices for agricultural commodities were rising, increasing the pressure on noble incomes, particularly those living on fixed rents.[51] At the same time, opportunities for commercial agriculture were growing; the incentive to take up farming for the market was strong. Commercially minded individuals among both English and French rural elites sought to increase the produce at their disposal and sell it. Both adopted sharp "business" practices: they were tough, efficient managers, keeping a sharp eye on the figures and a tight rein on their tenant farmers.[52] Their similarities end here, however. Whereas English landlords developed entirely new ways of appropriating a surplus, their French counterparts reanimated existing arrangements. In England, landowners began the process of enclosing and engrossing their farms: they evacuated the smaller peasants from their holdings, consolidated their lands and leased them to well-to-do tenant farmers on terms which permitted and induced them to develop the agricultural techniques that revolutionized production. In France, by contrast, the lords left the peasants in control of their small plots, using seigneurial levers to pump out an increasing share of their crop. The conditions of agriculture remained virtually unchanged: there were no important technical innovations. Clearly, the penetration of a commercial impulse into the countryside cannot by itself explain its transformation: the English and French nobility responded in diametrically opposed ways to the expansion of the market.

What, then, accounts for this difference? The advanced state of dissolution of feudal class relations in England as compared to France. That is, if the English landowners adopted wholly new methods of organizing land and labor to extract a surplus, they did so because the previous mode of exploitation had virtually collapsed. The option of obtaining a surplus by reasserting the manor's jurisdiction over the peasantry was closed off to them. There was no question of restoring the peasants' dependent status; villeinage had melted away. On the other side of the Channel, by contrast, the recovery of the seigneurie following the fourteenth century crisis permitted French lords to reassert feudal controls over the peasantry. Accordingly, their response to commercial agriculture took the form of a seigneurial reaction.

If the breakup of the manorial regime made it necessary for English landowners to search for alternative strategies of appropriating a surplus, the concomitant emancipation and disintegration of the village economy opened certain promising possibilities for doing so.[53] First, the loss of the peasants' capacity for class struggle facilitated their eviction from the soil. Hilton explains:

> English peasant communities in the thirteenth and fourteenth centuries had been capable of great resistance, even successful resistance, to attacks on their conditions by the landlords. If they allowed themselves to be evicted in the fifteenth and sixteenth centuries it was because economic and social changes had destroyed the cohesion that had been their strength in the past.[54]

Across the Channel, on the contrary, the French peasant communities, reanimated in their struggles with the lords for economic security and administrative autonomy, succeeded in entrenching themselves on the land.

Second, the economic dynamism engendered by the petty mode of production provided the lords with both the material means and the agents to reorganize agricultural production. The greater landowners supplied the land on which the husbandry practices pioneered by the well-to-do yeomen could be introduced on a larger scale; and the process of economic differentiation within the ranks of the direct producers supplied the lords with tenants capable of efficient farm management. Most of these employed wage labor. Thus, the elements set free by the dissolution of feudal society—the collapse of the manorial system and the consequent disintegration of the peasantry—recomposed themselves in the form of an emerging symbiotic relationship between landlord and tenant, a relationship that provided one of the principal foci in the making of the new dominant class.

In France, by contrast, increasing seigneurial pressure on the peasantry largely precluded both the improvement of agricultural production and the rise of a class of well-to-do farmers. Hence, even in those instances where seigneurs succeeded in enclosing and engrossing their farms, they typically lacked the option of leasing them to a big tenant and thus tended to divide it into small plots on which the cultivators continued to live as poor, increasingly wretched sharecroppers.

The English landowners did not, to be sure, make the transition to capitalist farming all at once; nor did all of them succeed in adapting to the new social configuration. Aristocrats who insisted on maintaining traditional levels of conspicuous consumption were usually forced to sell their lands or to seek royal favor to do so; many ended in ruin. Others, however, managed to balance their budgets by provident land sales, then took to rigorous exploitation of what was left in the new manner, thus recouping their fortunes.[55] Probably the leading edge of the classes altering the composition of the English countryside was to be found in that broad social swath below the peerage and above the yeomanry—that is, among the gentry. Again, however, there were gentlemen who stagnated and declined.[56] The transitory social formation was uniquely open: it was a combination of competing modes of production under the faltering dominance of one of them—feudalism. Not surprisingly, social and economic mobility was high.[57]

Studies focusing on the crisscrossing trajectories of family biographies have sometimes been adduced to demonstrate the inapplicability of the Marxian theory of class to interpret the nature of the social changes overtaking early modern England.[58] But the rise and fall of individual families need have little to do with the destiny of a *class*.[59] The argument being made here is that the *constellation* of possibilities for individual mobility was largely predetermined by the matrix of ownership relations. The available avenues of appropriating a surplus both conditioned and were conditioned by processes of class conflict and class formation. In England, the emerging property order induced considerable numbers among the landed classes to array themselves in opposition to the old regime, anchored in the twin institutions of Crown and Church.[60] Gentlemen who resorted to court connections as the path to windfall wealth typically found themselves in an increasingly tenuous position.[61] Similarly, the fact that the Civil War did not occasion any major redistribution of property from one group to another does not mean that the English class structure was not profoundly transformed by the Civil War.[62] If the land did not change hands, the *terms* on which individuals held it were fundamentally altered: the eighteenth century Whig oligarchy—in the main the descendants of England's natural rulers before the war—was no longer a class of lords but rather of capitalist landowners.[63]

In France, by contrast, the success of the absolute monarchy ensured the enforceability of the feudal property rights that formed the basis of the dominant class. It is hardly surprising, then, that the French nobility assembled itself around the Crown. Those lords who attempted to strike out independently and reorganize their estates in the English fashion came up against multiplying obstacles.[64] Thus, while the gentry rose to prominence in England, French property relations favored the rise of a wholly different class—the *noblesse de robe*, men of recent bourgeois extraction ennobled by the King. The Revolution would destroy the whole interlocking complex of aristocratic privilege. Again, to be sure, many French lords reentered France with the Bourbons to establish themselves among the leaders of the nineteenth century landed notables.[65] Nevertheless, it would be curious to argue that the nobility emerged victorious from the Revolution; those nobles who survived and prospered did so on the basis of entirely new class conditions.[66]

Capitalism and Productive Investment

The forcible expulsion of the rural population from the land radically transformed the social physiognomy of the English countryside. The emergent configuration of class relations took the form of the characteristic "three-tiered" structure of capitalist agriculture.[67] The rural capitalist was not one person but two: a big landlord, typically an aristocrat, who arranged the enclosures but left the details of estate management to a steward or agent, and a large tenant farmer, who made the actual economic contribution. The dispossessed peasants were reduced to proletarian status: they provided the necessary labor force required for a time to carry out the physical processes of enclosure and improvement or moved to the towns.

The logic of the new class system required the dominant class to adopt strategies for maximizing surplus appropriation which consisted primarily in productive investments. On the one hand, the market in tenants created by the introduction of short, terminable leases, and by the process of economic differentiation among the yeomanry, produced a situation in which all but the most efficient farmers went under.[68] The landlords sought to increase their revenues by raising rents, thus compelling the tenants to invest and improve their methods of cultivation to increase output and meet the higher rent charges, or be replaced by others capable and willing to take up the lease.[69] On the other hand, competition among landlords for tenants ensured that they could not simply "squeeze" the farmers, thereby threatening the funds available for improvement and hindering progressive husbandry. Indeed, "in order to compete for and to retain suitable tenants on their farms, landowners even felt obliged to subsidize outlays themselves."[70] The balance of market forces between landowners and tenants thus ensured a steady supply of resources to productive ends: "The shifting in their respective shares of estate management expenditure was . . . almost rhythmic."[71] The increasing flow of investment into the land raised "English agriculture from the rut of capital starvation in which the continental peasantry remained stuck."[72] The result was a process of rising agricultural productivity which allowed England to shake off the "dead hand of the 'crises of subsistence,' " which plagued precapitalist economies.[73]

Agricultural prosperity loosened the constraints which the inelasticity of the rural economy had traditionally imposed upon urban growth, permitting a gradual release of the factors of production into industry, and providing a home market for industrial products.[74] "As far as capital is concerned," writes L. A. Clarkson, "the agricultural sector was probably a net provider of capital to other sectors of the economy despite the fact that a good deal of mercantile wealth flowed into land."[75] Landlords and tenants were especially well placed to make big outlays in mining—coal, iron, copper, lead—usually an extension of the exploitation of the natural resources of their lands. They also invested heavily in laying the infrastructure of roads and canals.[76] Lastly, it seems that farmers made an important economic contribution by providing the entrepreneurial and technical skills necessary for raising the nascent manufactories: their sons shifted in considerable numbers to the towns to become apprentices.[77]

Enclosure and agricultural growth fueled productive development by providing a growing home market for commodities. The expropriation of the ordinary producers destroyed their self-sufficiency, raising the level of effective demand for industrial production.[78] As a result, the traditional economic antagonism between town and country was dissolved, replaced by an inceasingly symbiotic relationship: "each provided a market and ever cheaper means of production and consumption for the other."[79] Urban producers were principally consumers and processers of raw materials, which were supplied by the rural economy: "half a dozen crafts—textile, clothing, leather, metalworking, and the processing of food and drink—provided employment for roughly three-quarters of the urban workforce."[80] As manufacturing centers, the towns returned a flow of consumer goods to the countryside. The home market developed both quantitatively and qualitatively: rising prosperity, especially after 1650 when real wages started to rise, "resulted not only in an increased demand for commodities being consumed, but in a diversification of demand."[81] The purchase of industrial means of production by farmers, however, lagged far behind; the systematic application of machinery to agricultural production did not begin until the nineteenth century.

Capitalism and the Making of the Proletariat

The expropriation of the direct producers was at the core of the dynamic which created the industrial proletariat. In Marx's terms these years (roughly from 1550 to 1850) witnessed the "formal subjection" of labor to capital. That is, the ordinary producers, dispossessed of their means of production, were compelled to sell their labor power to capitalist employers in town and country. But the labor process in its technical aspects remained virtually unchanged. The early capitalist industries, either in the form of outwork or manufacture, depended largely on human powered production. Accordingly, although they were reduced to proletarian status, the workers rarely lost control over the work itself. The formal subjection of labor to capital, Marx argues, was the precondition to its "real subjection"—that is, to the process which assembled workers in factories, integrating them within mechanized production processes which usurped control over the rhythm of work.[82]

The relationship between the enclosure movement and the making of the industrial working class is highly contentious. Marxian theory maintains that the forcible expulsion of the peasant cultivators from their holdings was the main institutional means whereby the reserve army of labor requisite for capitalist industrial expansion was recruited.[83] This thesis has, however, come under serious criticism.[84] It is argued, first, that enclosure cannot have supplied a residual industrial workforce because enclosures very much tended to retain labor in agriculture, not expel it:

The newer systems of husbandry (especially the labour-intensive root breaks), the reclamation of barren land, and the physical processes of enclosure and improvement (hedging, in-fencing, building farms, and laying out accommodation roads) all demanded more labour, not less. . . . Apart from threshing machines, labour-saving machinery on the farm was unimportant before the nineteenth century.[85]

Secondly, agricultural and industrial work habits were not easily interchangeable, making the dispossessed cultivators poor "human material" for the new capitalist employers. Indeed, rural laborers were generally unwilling to exchange the security of the settlement for the vagaries of the industrial labor market; typically, only the young and the single emigrated. Industrial pursuits supplemented the family's agricultural production, or were the last refuge of rural poverty.[86] Lastly, the numerical increase in landless peasants released by enclosure was far too small and too sporadic to account for the increases in the industrial labor force in town and country.[87]

A counterhypothesis has emphasized the alternative explanation of natural demographic growth in providing "an entirely new supply of human material beside which the dislocations caused by enclosures were of secondary importance."[88] Maurice Dobb, however, objected that any assumption "that the appearance of a reserve army of labor was a simple product of growing population," implies that the "proletariat [was] a natural rather than an institutional creation, and . . . accumulation and the growth of a proletariat . . . [an] autonomous and independent processes."[89]

We should not, of course, unquestioningly accept the gloss his critics have put on Marx's account of the making of the proletariat. It is in many respects a caricature. Nowhere, for example, does Marx argue that the urban working class was simply recruited by the enclosures, in the sense that peasants were consciously dispossessed from their holdings and herded into waiting manufactories: he never entertained the proposition "that the enclosure commissioners were a kind of capitalist press gang."[90] Marx makes it quite clear that if the process of expulsion tended to mop up labor from the land, the rural workforce bitterly resisted being sucked into industry: the newly created proletarians, "suddenly dragged from their wonted mode of life, could not as suddenly adapt . . . to the discipline of their new condition."[91] Nevertheless, it remains true that Marx tended to be too simplistic about the extent to which the reserve army of labor was directly recruited by enclosure and eviction.

It seems clear that natural population growth was chiefly responsible for supplying the labor required by the expanding agricultural and manufacturing enterprises. But this is not to say, as Dobb believed, that "the proletariat [was] a natural rather than an institutional creation." For we have only to ask why the population increased in the first place, and why the multiplying numbers took the form of a growing *proletariat.* The answer lies in the twin facts that enclosure completed the destruction of peasant society, embodied in the traditional rural village, and occasioned improvements in agricultural productivity.

Traditional peasant communities had controlled the size of their population by requiring their youth to delay marriage. Permission to marry was linked to economic independence: young people were normally expected "to wait for positions in a village's economy to become vacant before they could marry and set up their own households."[92] Those who did not meet this qualification—for example, farmhands, maids—were expected to remain single. Similarly, urban artisans typically postponed marriage until they acquired sufficient capital to make themselves economically viable.[93] To be sure, this method of regulating the birth rate responded slowly to changing material circumstances. Thus, population growth beyond the resources of the village economy was punished by increases in the death rate. Still, in normal times, given the limited opportunities available in the rural economy, peasant communities succeeded in maintaining a rough demographic equilibrium in which each generation replaced its predecessor.

This equilibrium was undermined by the processes which expropriated the ordinary producers from the means of production.[94] First, expropriation removed the disincentive to marry early. Young men and women no longer had to wait until their fathers retired or died before setting up a household. In effect, they reached their full earning capacity at an early age, and thus had little reason to defer marriage. Lower age at marriage, of course, meant an increasing birth rate. Second, capitalist farming and manufacturing occasioned an economic expansion which not only supported an increase in the population as a whole, loosening the link between the economic cycle and the death rate, but more importantly in the proportion of the workforce which could devote itself to nonagricultural pursuits. Under the conditions of increasing employment opportunities, "the effect of a crumbling disincentive to early marriage made itself felt."[95] Lastly, the enclosure movement ensured that the option of life as autonomous cultivators and artisans was increasingly closed off to the vast majority of producers. The incentive to postpone marriage collapsed first and foremost amongst the most proletarianized sectors of the population, whose numbers thus increased faster than their more traditional brethren. The migration of urban industry to the countryside was given a prodigious stimulus by this growth: population pressure formed the backdrop for the rural relocation of industry. At the same time, the availability of cheap labor was one of the principal instruments whereby the new capitalist employers broke the independence of the artisans in the towns.[96]

THE BOURGEOIS REVOLUTIONS

The type of class struggle which culminated in the transfer of power from one class to another took the form of a clash between incompatible systems of surplus appropriation. The emergent capitalist class was obliged to complete the destruction of the feudal class relationship in order to clear the way for the reorganization of the methods by which an economic surplus could be extracted from the direct producers. To be sure, the internal composition of the transitory social formations was extremely complex: class struggles crisscrossed within and between types of exploitation. The bourgeois revolutions articulated and organized these clashes.

It has been frequently pointed out that the English and French Revolutions were fueled by two movements with divergent aims.[97] On the one hand, the ordinary producers in country and town struggled to secure an economy of simple commodity production. This was the central aim of the Levellers' economic program in England, and of the economic demands of the peasants and sansculottes in France.[98] On the other, the nascent capitalist class sought to sweep away the obstacles to the accumulation of property, that is, to abort the small producers' attempts to consolidate full ownership rights in their lands. This aim was reflected in the (ultimately successful) endeavor of the English Parliament to deny copyholders a security equivalent to freehold, and in the French Constituent Assembly's (only partially successful) attempts to indemnify landowners for the loss of the tithe and a panoply of feudal property rights.[99] Both revolutions were, of course, antifeudal. Both, therefore, could fuse in their opposition to the old order. Moreover, they found common ground in the emerging ideas of possessive individualism—that everyone had a property right in his goods and lands, including the right to own and accumulate by the exercise of his own energies and capacities—even if, of course, they interpreted these notions quite differently.[100]

This coalition of interests brought the feudal regime to a close. Indeed, as long as their interests converged, the radical revolution of the petty producers kept a fire under the revolution of the substantial property holders, forcing them to continue the work of dismantling the old order whenever the wealthy, never at ease with the idea of kicking over those aspects of the regime which protected property, vacillated.[101] But these two revolutions could work together and reinforce each other only up to a point, for they struggled to establish incompatible types of private property. The small producers sought to secure property rights restricted by social need and limited by the individual's own labor. The nascent capitalist class sought to secure unconditional and unlimited property rights, rights which rested on the employment of the labor of others. The latter, Marx pointed out, is "not only . . . the direct antithesis of the former, but absolutely grows on its tomb only."[102]

Marx argued that the bourgeois revolutions contained both an official and a secret history that designated them as bourgeois. The first recorded the movement which emancipated the direct producers "from serfdom and from the fetters of the guilds," completing the first precondition of capitalist accumulation. This history alone, he comments, "exists for our bourgeois historians." The second chronicled the realization of the second precondition, namely, the movement which "robbed [these new freedmen] of all their own means of production, and of all the guarantees of existence afforded by the old feudal arrangements. And the history of this, their expropriation, is written in the annals of mankind in letters of blood and fire."[103]

The thesis that England and France witnessed specifically "bourgeois" revolutions is the subject of much recent controversy. The sharpest criticism has been levelled against the notion that the revolutions were made by an increasingly independent bourgeoisie, commanding an ascendant capitalist economy, in the interest of displacing an established feudal aristocracy from the levers of political and social control. We are told that neither in pre-Civil War England nor in pre-Revolutionary France did there exist a mature bourgeois class, the product of capitalist development, clearly distinguishable from the nobility, whose members were increasingly resentful of existing arrangements which denied them a share of power commensurate with their economic position, and had a clear idea of the society they wished to bring into being.

In English historiography, this controversy took the form of a debate concerning R. H. Tawney's thesis that the transition from feudalism to capitalism could be understood in terms of "the rise of the gentry."[104] Some have questioned the equation of the gentry, a privileged landed class, with the bourgeoisie, a denomination purportedly reserved solely to the leaders of commerce and industry in the towns. As for the wealthy merchant oligarchies, it is argued that they were selfishly neutral or sided with the Crown as the guarantor of their economic privileges; and many who entered the countryside tended to assimilate themselves to the conditions of life of the nobility, not to transform rural relations into capitalist relations. Moreover, the gentry was a fragmented and not a homogeneous class: economically, while many gentry were rising, many were declining; politically, they were either divided or neutral. Whether the entrepreneurial, commercially oriented, "bourgeois" gentry sided with the Parliament and the paternalistic, rentier, "feudal" gentry sided with the king is a suggestive hypothesis but open to question. Furthermore, it is plain enough that the gentry was not a self-conscious, revolutionary class; it did not view the existing regime with increasing resentment. Indeed, most gentlemen struggled to preserve it, endeavoring until the very last to make the system work. When it came, the Revolution caught them unawares: they more or less stumbled on to it. Certainly very few if any intended it.

In French historiography, the controversy over what fundamentally changed and how in the Revolution can be traced to Alfred Cobban's critical review of George Lefebvre's interpretation.[105] Recent research has cast much doubt on the idea that the bourgeoisie formed an economically and socially distinct class in conflict with the nobility. Rather, commercial and financial wealth existed symbiotically with "proprietary," that is, feudal, forms of wealth. It cannot be argued, therefore, that existing arrangements were thwarting middle class aspirations, goading them into opposition to the ancien regime. The bourgeoisie did not suffer from an increasing sense of indignity at the hands of the monarchy and aristocracy: they did not, in short, possess a revolutionary class consciousness. Nor did they possess the capacity to make a revolution, for they were not a homogeneous but a diverse class, internally divided by multiple layers of privilege and occupation. Indeed, the revolutionaries were not capitalist entrepreneurs but lawyers, officers and intellectuals. Nor were the men who dominated France after the Revolution capitalist entrepreneurs but bureaucrats, soldiers and above all landowners. Perhaps most telling against the Marxist interpretation is that the Revolution proved not to be conducive to capitalist industry, but rather hindered it. The finding that the industrial bourgeoisie did not profit from the revolution is adduced to question the thesis that they made it.

Marx's detractors frequently preface their criticisms with the complaint that he attempts to fit complex historical events into a preconceived philosophy of history. The problem is that his critics all too often have a preconceived idea of Marx's theory into which they fit his actual historical analyses. The notion that Marx postulated a homogeneous, preformed class of capitalist entrepreneurs armed with a clear blueprint of the society they wished to construct may be their interpretation of Marx, but it is certainly not his interpretation of the bourgeois revolutions.[106]

The claim that the revolutions were carried out according to the wishes of individuals fully conscious of their membership in a rising class is alien to Marx's historical studies. He recognizes that the old order inhibited the formation of an active self-awareness of class identity. The objective socioeconomic basis of class was complicated by an ensemble of particularistic, corporate groupings which fragmented class identification.[107] Needless to say, the interlocking complex of privilege contained a concrete economic meaning: its core was the dominant class's enforceable claims to extract an economic surplus from the direct producers. But this economic foundation was concealed by the juridical forms in which it was cast. It is important to recall that both the "gentry" and the "bourgeoisie" were defined by law; economically, they were divided.[108] To be sure, the official regime of private jurisdictions was beginning to disintegrate as a result of changes in the configuration of class relations.[109] But the struggles and conflicts in which these changes manifested themselves were still mediated by the system of estates and prerogatives that governed legal and political relations.[110] Furthermore, Marx maintains that revolutionary solidarity required the *suppression* of a particular class identity. But if the revolutionary leaders lacked a clear consciousness of their class, this is not to say that they lacked any form of class consciousness. Rather, they found in the language of the past—the English in the Bible, the French in republican Rome—"the self-deceptions that they needed in order to conceal from themselves the bourgeois limitations of the content of their struggles and to maintain their passion on the high plane of great historical tragedy."[111] Lastly, Marx argues that the revolutionary leaders were forced to speak in this borrowed language precisely because they were entering an alien world, unsure of their historical bearings.[112]

The equation of capitalism with the factory system is likewise not Marx's. The distinction between the two has been reiterated frequently enough in these pages not to need belaboring again. The capitalist mode of production refers to a system of class relations specifying the way in which wealth is appropriated from the immediate producers. Capitalism, then, *preceded* industrialization; the strategies the class system obliged the dominant class to adopt to maximize surplus appropriation corresponded to an unprecedented degree with the requirements for developing the productive forces. Nor does Marx dogmatically equate the capitalist class with the upper strata of the towns, making rural capitalism a contradiction in terms. On the contrary, we have seen that he both underscored the conservative nature of merchant capitalism and maintained that the transition to the capitalist mode of production occurred first in the countryside, not in the cities. Indeed, he emphasized that the progress of industry necessarily rested mainly upon prosperity in agriculture.

The feudal regime did not, then, collapse as the result of a planned assault upon it by a class-conscious industrial bourgeoisie. Rather, as we have seen, it disintegrated from *within*. The crisis complex manifested itself first in a paralysis of the Crown, as the institutional cornerstone of the whole structure. The crisis was the unintended and unwanted result of prior processes of class struggle; its emergence took the main classes by surprise. Its *resolution*, however, depended upon the active intervention of the contending classes, in which their different capacities for struggle were forced to the fore, and the concrete historical options available to them were thrown into bold relief.[113] The bourgeois revolutions, as it were, provided the crucible in which the elements set free by the process of disintegration of the old order were welded together to form the new. This process forged the disparate fractions of the bourgeoisie into a national ruling class.

This interpretation is in two crucial respects precisely the opposite of the view his critics have assigned to Marx. First, the revolutions occurred not at the culmination but at the inception of the process of formation of the capitalist class: They cannot be understood to be the result of a preformed bourgeoisie. In an important sense, the bourgeoisie as a class is the result of the revolutions.[114] Secondly, neither can the revolutions be understood as the product of industrial development. Rather, their significance lies at the level of property relations—enforceable claims to the use and benefit of labor power and productive resources—which constituted the system of exploitation. Their special accomplishment was to "sweep away" the ruins of a rapidly disintegrating regime, "clogged by all manner of medieval rubbish," thus removing the barriers to a reorganization of the economy and society according to the universal principles of private property and equality before the law.[115] They were *bourgeois* in the specific sense that they simplified and consolidated the complex array of particularistic and arbitrary corporate privileges into a single, individual property right. The characteristic feudal mode of surplus appropriation was thereby permanently abolished, replaced by juridical conditions which made both necessary and possible the capitalist mode of appropriation.[116]

The bourgeois revolutions did not, needless to say, assume the same configuration in England and France: The major contrast between them was the product of differences in the relative strength of the competing class systems in the two countries. The English peasantry's early success in crippling the manorial regime resulted in an extensive dissolution of feudal class relations, permitting an unprecedented consolidation of capitalist class relations.[117] On the one hand, by the seventeenth century the direct producers in both town and country formed a markedly differentiated class.[118] Their capacity for concerted action was rapidly melting away. On the other, the central fact of the English Crown was its deficiency in the essential components of absolutist power—money, bureaucracy, army. By 1640, the Stuart monarchy was unable to continue governing in the traditional way: the Scottish invasion occasioned its virtual paralysis.

This is the social setting which both compelled and permitted the emergent capitalist landlords to remake the institutions of the old order in a form suited to their requirements. This is not to say that a class conscious revolutionary party controlled the Commons. The breakdown of the government caught the parliamentary leaders largely by surprise; their immediate response was to try to make the system work. But the crisis presented them with certain stark choices.[119] On the one hand, cooperation with the government would exact too high a price, in the form of an extension of the Crown's sphere of the "prerogative," which threatened the landlords' property rights. On the other, accession to the radicals' demands for the security of copyhold tenure would equally undermine their control over the land. These twin dangers tended to polarize and split the landed classes. What allowed the parliamentary leaders to steer a "middle path" was, precisely, the weakness of the traditional class structure. The economic divisions within the ranks of the direct producers both induced the landowners to rely on popular protest to challenge the monarchy's authority, and enabled them to defeat radical property demands. The Levellers, in effect, articulated the interests of a class that was disappearing from the historical stage; the decade of the 1640s witnessed the beginning of the end of the yeomanry as a cohesive social force. The parish elites, composed principally of rising, commercially oriented yeomen farmers, followed and pressed the larger landlords to complete the transformation of the existing regime. The rest, the mass of the poor, were eliminated from English political life. The gentry thus retained its leadership at the vital turning point of the revolution, "when the fighting was over [and] the Leveller democratic organization gave a dangerous political significance to what had hitherto been spontaneous activities."[120]

The result was an institutional framework which facilitated capitalist development. The parliamentary leaders abolished wardship and the Court of Wards, converting all lands that were formerly held of the king by feudal tenure into absolute ownership.[121] At the same time, "feudal tenures were abolished upwards only, not downwards."[122] The Parliament brought down the prerogative courts by which the Crown had sought to protect smallholders from eviction. In fact, both King and Parliament had fitfully sought to stem enclosures prior to the Civil War. Enclosure had been pushed forward mainly by individual improving lords. After 1660, no government seriously attempted to check them. Rather, they were now arranged by the Parliament itself.[123] Copyholders lost all attempts to secure property rights in their holdings; most obstacles to enclosure were thus removed. Whatever was restored at the Restoration, it is clear that feudal tenures and restraints upon the enclosure of land were not.[124] By the eighteenth century, the enclosure movement in England experienced a veritable boom, reaching its climax during the Napoleonic Wars.[125] "The rise of a landless proletariat was a long drawn out process;" Christopher Hill commented, "but henceforth it was an inevitable one."[126]

The French Revolution, by contrast, was determined by the *conjuncture* of class struggles within and between class systems.

Unlike their English counterparts, the French peasants, as we have seen, still formed a coherent class on the eve of the Revolution. Indeed, it is clear that the peasants, not the bourgeoisie, played the decisive role in what is surely the single most important achievement of the Revolution—the dismantling of feudalism.[127] Yet it is equally clear that the victory of the peasants showed, as the victory of their counterparts across the Channel had shown two centuries earlier, the intrinsic limits of village solidarity.[128] The French peasants were already some way along in the process of internal differentiation. Against the seigneurs, their common enemy, they maintained their unity; in nearly every other respect, large and small holders were divided.[129] Their cohesion made the Revolution possible; but their very success in removing the seigneurs destroyed their rationale for concerted action and allowed their divergent interests to acquire an increasingly preponderant weight in their actions. "What happened," writes R. R. Palmer, "was that during the Revolution the peasant bloc, the communal village, agrarian solidarity, were broken. Never again could there be a universal agrarian upheaval as in 1789."[130] In other words, the destruction of the seigneurial regime was the beginning of the end of the peasantry as a cohesive social force. This fact explains one of the most ironic aspects of the peasants' contribution to the Revolution: Whereas they were chiefly responsible for abolishing the seigneurial regime, they failed to achieve any substantial redistribution of land in their favor. Very little land changed hands, and no more than half of that went to the peasants, mostly to the well-to-do among them.[131] If the Revolution was the work of the peasantry, only its wealthier members reaped any benefits.

Whereas the elimination of the feudal mode of exploitation was the accomplishment of the class struggle within the ancien regime, it was the antagonism between class systems which replaced it with the regime of private property. To be sure, the bourgeois members of the Third Estate showed no penchant for revolution prior to 1789.[132] Rather, they had traditionally sought to find a place within the nobility. But the progressive sclerosis of the ancien regime made entry into it increasingly difficult, especially for bourgeoisie further down in the channels of promotion. The question of the exclusiveness of the nobility came to a head in 1788, when the Parlement of Paris decided that the Estates General would meet in its seventeenth century form, in effect arbitrarily banishing from noble status substantial numbers of the bourgeoisie. The latter, of course, balked, although, again, their main interest was to preserve the existing institutions, albeit in a mode which permitted freer entry.

But the quarrels within the dominant class sparked the revolution from below, that is, the uprising of the peasantry and the sansculotterie, presenting the leaders of the bourgeoisie with certain stark choices. They could endeavor to restore the traditional order, systematically repressing popular unrest, or embark on a wholly new path, leading to a radical transformation of the regime. Unlike its English counterpart, however, the French bourgeoisie could not steer a path between cooperation with the monarchy and accession to popular demands. The very strength of the contending classes constituting the ancien regime did not permit it to do so. The result was a dynamic of increasing political polarization within the ranks of the bourgeoisie. On the one hand, its more conservative members began to draw closer to the Crown in an attempt to defeat popular revolts by reviving the apparatus of absolutism they had sought to reform. On the other, its liberal members were pushed further into the opposition, increasingly distrustful of the King and fearful of counter-revolution, ultimately ratifying not only the peasantry's de facto abolition of seigneurialism, but revamping most of the institutions of the ancien regime besides. In effect, it was the pressure of popular rebellion that *made* the bourgeoisie, compelling its leaders to break its subaltern dependence on the old order, to disavow its participation in the traditional forms of wealth (during the famous night of August 4, 1789), and to begin the arduous and protracted process of constituting the nascent class into a national ruling class.[133] Their singular achievement, which imparted to the Revolution its bourgeois character, was to transform the bewildering complex of feudal property rights into the absolute right of private property.

It must be emphasized, however, that the specific conjuncture of class struggles that characterized the French Revolution would hinder industrial development. Although its participation in the Revolution was its last major initiative as a class, the peasantry did exact a final price: the same laws the bourgeoisie designed to protect private property confirmed the peasants' rights to their holdings. Thus, even though the agricultural revolution left the peasants internally divided and with a diminished capacity for united action against the emergent capitalist class, their eventual eviction from the soil would be accomplished more slowly than in England. Thus, the distinctive processes of class conflict and class formation which attended the transition to capitalism in France hindered its economic development well into the nineteenth century.[134]

NOTES

1. Marx, Vol. 1 of *Capital,* p. 667.
2. Ibid., pp. 668–69.
3. Ibid., p. 165.
4. Ibid.
5. Ibid., p. 166; see also p. 669.
6. Cf. Marx, *Manifesto of the Communist Party,* in Vol. 6 of Marx and Engels, *Collected Works,* p. 482. (Hereafter *CW.*)
7. Marx, *Capital* 1:668. This is also Dobb's thesis: see *Studies in the Development of Capitalism,* p. 20.
8. Marx, *Capital* 1:703; Letter to N. K. Mikhailovsky, November 1877, in *Selected Correspondence,* p. 293.
9. On the dissolution of demesne cultivation, see Postan, *The Medieval Economy and Society,* pp. 75, 106–08; Hilton, *The Decline of Serfdom in Medieval England,* pp. 44–45, and *The English Peasantry in the Later Middle Ages,* p. 60.
10. See, for example, Hilton, *The Decline of Serfdom in Medieval England,* pp. 32–43, and *The English Peasantry in the Later Middle Ages,* pp. 58–73; Postan, *The Medieval Economy and Society,* pp. 151–54; Anderson, *Passages from Antiquity to Feudalism,* pp. 206–07.
11. On the evolution of peasant land tenure in late medieval England, see Hilton, *The Decline of Serfdom in Medieval England,* pp. 44–51; Clarkson, *The Pre-Industrial Economy in England,* pp. 63–66; Brenner, "The Agrarian Roots of European Capitalism," in *The Brenner Debate,* ed. Aston and Philpin, pp. 293–299.
12. Marx, *Capital* 1:671.
13. Marx, *Capital* 3:798.

14. Ibid.

15. Ibid.

16. Hilton, *The Decline of Serfdom in Medieval England,* p. 45.

17. Postan, *The Medieval Economy and Society,* p. 140.

18. Marx, *Grundrisse,* p. 510. "Golden age" is also the term Postan uses to describe the economic condition of the peasantry at the close of the Middle Ages. See *The Medieval Economy and Society,* p. 142.

19. Postan, *The Medieval Economy and Society,* pp. 139–41; Hilton, *The English Peasantry in the Later Middle Ages,* pp. 39–40.

20. Marx, *Capital* 1:713, and *Capital* 3:806–07.

21. Hilton's studies in *The English Peasantry in the Later Middle Ages* formed part of an attempt to delineate the physiognomy of the petty mode of production. See his introductory remarks, pp. 18–19. The importance of an unfettered peasantry in promoting agricultural development was also stressed by Patricia Croot and David Parker, "Agrarian Class Structure and the Development of Capitalism: France and England Compared," in *The Brenner Debate,* ed. Aston and Philpin, pp. 79–81, 85, 87–89.

22. Hilton offers much of the best discussion of this process of internal disintegration in *The English Peasantry in the Late Middle Ages,* pp. 161–73.

23. Hilton, *The English Peasantry in the Later Middle Ages,* p. 51.

24. Hilton, *Bond Men Made Free,* pp. 34–35.

25. Hilton, *The English Peasantry in the Later Middle Ages,* p. 51.

26. The last peasant rising in England was in 1549; the rural poor were almost wholly quiescent during the Civil War. See Stone, *The Causes of the English Revolution,* pp. 54–55, 76–77.

27. Hilton, "A Crisis of Feudalism," in *The Brenner Debate,* ed. Aston and Philpin, p. 135.

28. Hill, *Reformation to Industrial Revolution,* p. 70.

29. Ibid., p. 120.

30. Hilton, "A Crisis of Feudalism," pp. 133–135; Croot and Parker, pp. 79–81; A. R. Bridbury, *Economic Growth, England in the Later Middle Ages,* Ch. 6, esp. pp. 89–92.

31. Marx, *Capital* 1:799.

32. Brenner underscores the crucial role played by the disintegration of the peasantry in clearing the way for capitalistic accumulation. "Agrarian Class Structure and Economic Development," in *The Brenner Debate,* ed. Aston and Philpin, pp. 30, 48–55. In their review of this article, Croot and Parker emphasize the critical contribution of the peasantry to agricultural productivity. "Agrarian Class Structure," pp. 79–88. The argument being made here is that these twin devel-

opments were intrinsically interwoven, and that both were necessary prerequisites of the rise of capitalist production.

33. A detailed explanation of this divergence is beyond the scope of this study. Marxist historians have argued that the very precocity of ruling class organization in England "froze" the development of the feudal monarchy in a form which, albeit highly successful in the Middle Ages, proved unable to withstand the stress of the general crisis of the fourteenth century. By contrast, the French monarchy began its process of centralization in large measure as a response to the crisis and its aftermath. Ironically, this late development permitted it "to reorganize and recompose the French ruling class on a stronger basis." Brenner, "The Agrarian Roots of European Capitalism" in *The Brenner Debate*, ed. Aston and Philpin, p. 263. Brenner's discussion of this issue appears on pp. 253–64. See also Anderson, *Lineages of the Absolutist State*, pp. 85–142; Hilton, *The Decline of Serfdom in Medieval England*, p. 16. Cf. Bloch, *French Rural History*, pp. 126–29.

34. Guy Bois, *The Crisis of Feudalism*, p. 407.

35. Goubert, *The Ancien Regime*, pp. 185–86, 188–91.

36. Bloch, *French Rural History*, p. 125. This and the following paragraph rely heavily on Bloch's discussion of the reconstruction of the seigneurie: Ibid., pp. 123–35. See also, Le Roy Ladurie, *The Peasants of Languedoc*, pp. 93–94, 142–44, 213–16, 292; Kriedte, *Peasants, Landlords and Merchant Capitalists*, pp. 24–25, 92–93, 108–09, 111.

37. See Goubert, *The Ancien Regime*, pp. 82–87, 122–34; Lefebvre, *The Coming of the French Revolution*, pp. 135–42; Kriedte, pp. 92–93. The terms "feudal" and "seigneurial" are surrounded by controversy, carrying a bewildering number of connotations. I am using the notion of feudalism in its strict Marxist sense to indicate a particular historical mode of surplus extraction. The distinguishing characteristic of this mode is the seigneurie or manor. See the discussion above, Chapter 3, Class Structure. See also Anderson, *Lineages*, pp. 401–10. Despite changes in its form, the seigneurie remained a powerful institution until its suppression by the French Revolution. Indeed there was much less ambiguity in the historical experience of the contending classes themselves than among contemporary historians. Both the Constituent Assembly, on the celebrated night of August 4, 1789, and especially the peasants, equated the ancien regime with feudalism, and the latter with the seigneurial system. For the peasants, the seigneurial regime was a living reality, and its memory aroused bitter hatred well into the nineteenth century. Lefebvre, *The Coming of the French Revolution*, pp. 137–39, 155–68; Goubert, *The Ancien Regime*, pp. 1–15; Albert Soboul, "Persistence of 'Feudalism' in the Rural Society of Nineteenth-

Century France," in *Rural Society in France*, ed. Robert Forster and Orest Ranum, trans. Elborg Forster and Patricia M. Ranum (Baltimore: The Johns Hopkins University Press, 1977), pp. 65–71.

38. Goubert, *The Ancien Regime*, p. 78.

39. Bloch, *French Rural History*, pp. 116, 128–29.

40. Anderson, *Lineages*, p. 25.

41. See Bloch, *French Rural History*, pp. 143–44; Goubert, *The Ancien Regime*, pp. 127, 136, 159.

42. Goubert, *The Ancien Regime*, p. 127.

43. Ibid., p. 102.

44. The contrast drawn below develops suggestions made by Croot and Parker, pp. 83–89.

45. Goubert, *The Ancien Regime*, p. 136.

46. Ibid., p. 137.

47. Ibid., pp. 103–15. See also Lefebvre, *The Great Fear*, pp. 7–13.

48. Goubert, *The Ancien Regime*, pp. 36–42; Le Roy Ladurie, *The Peasants of Languedoc*, p. 310.

49. Marx, *Capital* 1:668.

50. See Brenner, "The Agrarian Roots of European Capitalism," pp. 303–06.

51. See Bloch, *French Rural History*, pp. 121–23; Hill, *Reformation to Industrial Revolution*, pp. 61–62, 82–83; Clarkson, pp. 32–35.

52. See Goubert, *The Ancien Regime*, pp. 174, 177–78; Bloch, *French Rural History*, pp. 123–26; Moore, *Social Origins of Dictatorship and Democracy*, pp. 5–7, 14–15, 52–56; Hill, *Reformation to Industrial Revolution*, pp. 65–68, 83; Braudel, *The Wheels of Commerce*, pp. 294–97; Kriedte, 111.

53. The principal source for this argument is Brenner, "The Origins of Capitalist Development," pp. 77–78.

54. Hilton, *The English Peasantry in the Later Middle Ages*, p. 173. Cf. Marx, *Capital* 1:474. Brenner misses this point. He explains the inception of the enclosure movement by arguing, somewhat inconsistently, that the English lords were both too weak to restore the lordship in the class struggles unleashed by the general feudal crisis, and yet strong enough to begin the process of evicting the peasants from the soil. On the other side of the class divide, he maintains that the peasant communities were sufficiently cohesive to put an end to serfdom, and yet failed to retain control over their lands. The lacuna in this argument can be filled by examining the dynamics of class cohesion and disintegration within the peasantry, something he neglects to do. See especially "The Agrarian Roots of European Capitalism," pp. 271–72, 291–99.

55. See Tawney, "The Rise of the Gentry 1558–1640," p. 181; Hill, *Reformation to Industrial Revolution*, pp. 65–68; Stone, *The Causes of the English Revolution*, pp. 30, 83–84; Moore, pp. 14–15.

56. See Tawney, "The Rise of the Gentry," pp. 186–88; Hill, *Reformation to Industrial Revolution*, pp. 29–31, 64–66; Stone, *The Causes of the English Revolution*, pp. 72–75; Moore, pp. 15–16; Perez Zagorin, "The Social Interpretation of the English Revolution," pp. 379–80.

57. See Stone, *The Causes of the English Revolution*, pp. 110–11; Hill, *Reformation to Industrial Revolution*, pp. 127–28.

58. The battle was occasioned by Tawney's thesis that the English economy and society underwent a transition from feudalism to capitalism which can be understood in terms of the rise of the gentry. We shall explore this debate more fully below in the third section of this chapter, The Bourgeois Revolutions.

59. See Christopher Hill, "Recent Interpretations of the Civil War," in *Puritanism and Revolution*, pp. 8–11, and "A Bourgeois Revolution?" in *Three British Revolutions*, ed. Pocock, pp. 111, 124–25.

60. Christopher Hill, "Parliament and People in Seventeenth Century England," pp. 107–15.

61. Hill, *Reformation to Industrial Revolution*, p. 67.

62. See Stone, *The Causes of the English Revolution*, p. 49; Moore, p. 18.

63. See Hill, *Reformation to Industrial Revolution*, pp. 146–48.

64. Brenner, "The Agrarian Roots of European Capitalism," pp. 312–314; Bloch, *French Rural History*, pp. 218, 219, 222–23; Moore, pp. 62, 63–69.

65. The French Revolution, like its English predecessor, produced little redistribution of landownership. See Theda Skocpol, *States and Social Revolutions*, p. 126.

66. Fox-Genovese and Genovese, *Fruits of Merchant Capital*, p. 225.

67. See Marx, *Capital* 1:694, and *Capital* 3:799.

68. Hill, *Reformation to Industrial Revolution*, p. 154.

69. Clarkson, pp. 67–68; Brenner, "Origins of Capitalist Development," p. 76; Croot and Parker, p. 85.

70. E. L. Jones, "Agriculture and Economic Growth in England, 1660–1750," in *Agriculture and Economic Growth in England, 1650–1815*, p. 160. See also his "Editor's Introduction" to this work, pp. 14–15.

71. Jones, "Agriculture and Economic Growth in England," p. 160.

72. Jones, "Editor's Introduction," p. 14.

73. Ibid., p. 18. See also Brenner, "Origins of Capitalist Development," p. 77, and "The Agrarian Roots of European Capitalism," in

The Brenner Debate, ed. Aston and Philpin, pp. 317–319; Marx, *Capital* 1:697.

74. See Marx, *Capital* 1:697–99.

75. Clarkson, p. 71. See also Jones, "Editor's Introduction," pp. 25–26.

76. Jones, "Editor's Introduction," p. 32.

77. Ibid., pp. 27ff.

78. See Marx, *Capital* 1:699–700; Clarkson, pp. 47–48; Hill, *Reformation to Industrial Revolution*, pp. 246–49; Kriedte, pp. 77, 116–17, 131.

79. Brenner, "Origins of Capitalist Development," p. 77. See also Peter Clark, "Introduction: English Country Towns 1500–1800," in *Country Towns in Pre-Industrial England*, pp. 17–19.

80. Clarkson, p. 80.

81. Ibid., p. 72. See also Jones, "Editor's Introduction," p. 42.

82. Marx, *Capital* 1:476–79. Kriedte, following modern usage, refers to this stage in the transition from the family workshop to the factory system as protoindustrial (see pp. 165–66, 174, 180–82).

83. Ibid., 669, 672–85.

84. See, e.g., Jones, "Editor's Introduction," pp. 21–25; J. D. Chambers, "Enclosure and Labor Supply in the Industrial Revolution," in *Agriculture and Economic Growth in England, 1650–1815*.

85. Jones, "Editor's Introduction," pp. 21–22.

86. Ibid., p. 24.

87. Chambers, "Labor Supply in the Industrial Revolution," pp. 120, 122–23.

88. Ibid., pp. 120–21.

89. Dobb, *Studies in the Development of Capitalism*, p. 223.

90. Jones, "Editor's Introduction," p. 21.

91. Marx, *Capital* 1:686.

92. David Levine, *Family Formation in an Age of Nascent Capitalism*, p. 45. See also pp. 11, 148; Kriedte, p. 19.

93. Levine, p. 51.

94. This discussion relies primarily on Levine, pp. 11–12, 45–46, 51–52, 58–87, 147–48.

95. Ibid., p. 148.

96. See Thompson, *The Making of the English Working Class*, pp. 259–346.

97. See, for example, Hill, *The Century of Revolution*, pp. 161–64; Skocpol, pp. 64–67, 181–85; Lefebvre, *The Coming of the French Revolution*, pp. 158–61, 212–14; Moore, pp. 16–19, 77–79, 83–84.

98. On England, see Macpherson, *The Political Theory of Possessive*

Individualism, pp. 154–58. On France, see Skocpol, pp. 126–28; Lefebvre, *The Coming of The French Revolution*, pp. 134–35, 212–13, 218; Moore, pp. 71–74, Albert Soboul, "Classes and Class Struggles During the French Revolution," pp. 250–52.

99. On the English Parliament, see Hill, *Reformation to Industrial Revolution*, pp. 146–48, and *The Century of Revolution*, pp. 126–27; Macpherson, pp. 112–14. On the French Constituent Assembly, see Lefebvre, *The Coming of The French Revolution*, pp. 155–68; Soboul, "Persistence of 'Feudalism' in the Rural Society of Nineteenth-Century France," pp. 51–61, and *passim*.

100. Macpherson, pp. 262–71. For an account of the conflicts that divided substantial bourgeois property holders from petty producers in France see Lefebvre, *The Coming of the French Revolution*, pp. 47–49, 106, 141–42, 155–68, 213–14; Soboul, "Classes and Class Struggles During the French Revolution," pp. 249–52, and *The Parisian Sans-Culottes and the French Revolution 1793–4*, pp. 18–98; Moore, pp. 71–74, 83–84, 104. We are referring principally to the more prosperous peasants and artisans. The poorer sort, to the extent that they made their presence felt, provided the social basis for the most radical demands voiced during the revolutions—the program of the Diggers in England, the *loi agraire* in France. This split, more pronounced in England, less so in France, was the political expression of the process of differentiation within their ranks.

101. See Marx, "Moralising Criticism and Critical Morality," *CW* 6:319–20, and "The Bourgeoisie and the Counter-Revolution," *CW* 8:161–62. See also Hill, "Parliament and People in Seventeenth Century England," pp. 109–13, 118–21, and "A Bourgeois Revolution?" pp. 115, 133; Skocpol, pp. 183–85; Moore, pp. 77–79, 83–84, 104.

102. Marx, *Capital* 1:716.

103. Ibid., p. 669.

104. R. H. Tawney, "The Rise of the Gentry, 1558–1640," pp. 173–214. The equation of the gentry with the bourgeoisie was criticized, among others, by J. H. Hexter, *Reappraisals in History*, ch. 5; Zagorin, pp. 389–92; Stone, *The Causes of the English Revolution*, pp. 39–40. The fact that there existed "rising" and "falling" gentlemen, and that their loyalties were either neutral or divided is a commonplace in the literature: see, for example, Zagorin, pp. 389–94; Stone, *The Causes of the English Revolution*, pp. 55–56, 74–75. Trevor-Roper maintained that the condition of the gentry as a whole declined during this period. "The Gentry, 1540–1640," pp. 1–55. This was the first assault upon Tawney's argument, which opened the debate. Trevor-Roper's counterhypothesis itself came under serious criticism by Zagorin, pp. 378–

87, and Hill, "Recent Interpretations of the Civil War," pp. 6–14. A forceful defense of the "bourgeois revolution" thesis was recently given by Hill, "Parliament and People in Seventeenth Century England," pp. 100–24, and "A Bourgeois Revolution?" pp. 109–39, and challenged in equally forceful terms by A. J. Fletcher: see their exchange in the pages of *Past and Present*, 98 (February 1983): 151–58. See also Stone, "The Bourgeois Revolution of Seventeenth Century England Revisited," pp. 44–54. A good analysis of the controversy is provided by Stone, *The Causes of the English Revolution*, ch. 2.

105. See Cobban, *The Social Interpretation of the French Revolution*. See also Taylor, "Types of Capitalism in Eighteenth Century France," pp. 478–97, and "Non-Capitalist Wealth and the Origins of the French Revolution," pp. 469–96; Colin Lucas, "Nobles, Bourgeois and the Origins of the French Revolution," in Johnson, ed., *French Society and the Revolution*, pp. 98–131. For Lefebvre's analysis of the shifting class patterns on the eve of the Revolution, see *The Coming of the French Revolution*. A brief statement of the "bourgeois revolution" thesis is provided by Soboul, "Classes and Class Struggles During the French Revolution," pp. 238–57. The debate is ably summarized by Skocpol in *States and Social Revolutions*, pp. 174–77. A spirited review of this controversy, from a Marxist perspective, is offered by Fox-Genovese and Genovese, ch. 8.

106. It is worth noting that the critics of the Marxist interpretation of the bourgeois revolutions have typically aimed their fire at the interpretation of Marx's followers and only beyond them at Marx himself. It is true that Marx's own account has often suffered more at the hands of his epigones than at the hands of his critics. The interpretation offered in these pages seeks to reconstruct Marx's historical studies while at the same time relying on such great Marxist historians as Christopher Hill and Georges Lefebvre.

107. See, for example, Marx, *Manifesto of the Communist Party*, *CW* 6:482–85.

108. See Hill, "Recent Interpretations of the Civil War," p. 8; Fox-Genovese and Genovese, pp. 223–27. Cf. Marx, "Moralising Criticism and Critical Morality," *CW* 6:337.

109. A revealing account of this process is provided by Robert Darnton in an analysis of the changing *mentalités* of mid-eighteenth century France, in *The Great Cat Massacre*. Chapter 3 of this book is a study of "a description of Montpellier written in 1768 by an anonymous but solidly middle-class citizen of the city." (p. 107) What is interesting in this description is the way in which this bourgeois *de l'ancien régime* attempts to square the traditional categories of social

stratification—dignities, estates—with the shifting class patterns of eighteenth century France, and in the process strains them to the breaking point: "But the language of estates was no more modern than the language of dignities. Our author used an antiquated set of categories, emptied them of their old meanings, and rearranged them in such a way as to convey the shape of a social order like the one that would emerge openly in the nineteenth century. . . . "(p. 126)

110. Fox-Genovese and Genovese, pp. 223–27, 229–37; Hill "A Bourgeois Revolution?" p. 129–31.

111. Marx, *The Eighteenth Brumaire of Louis Bonaparte*, *CW* 11:104–05.

112. Ibid., pp. 103–05.

113. See Hill, "Parliament and People in Seventeenth Century England," pp. 109–13, and "A Bourgeois Revolution?" pp. 111, 130–31; Skocpol, pp. 183–85; Fox-Genovese and Genovese, pp. 225–27.

114. See Hill, "A Bourgeois Revolution?" p. 110; Lucas, "Nobles, Bourgeois and the Origins of the French Revolution," in *French Society and the Revolution*, ed. O. Johnson, p. 130.

115. Marx, *The Civil War in France*, in *The Marx-Engels Reader*, pp. 629–30. For Marx's characterization of the specific accomplishment of the English Civil War, see *Capital* 1:676, 677–78.

116. See Skocpol, p. 179, Fox-Genovese and Genovese, p. 224. Perhaps the best summary of this view is provided by Isaac Deutscher: "The traditional view, widely accepted by Marxists and anti-Marxists alike, is that in such revolutions, in Western Europe, the bourgeoisie played the leading part, stood at the head of the insurgent people, and seized power. . . . It seems to me that this conception, to whatever authorities it may be attributed, is schematically and historically unreal. . . . Capitalist entrepreneurs, merchants and bankers were not conspicuous among the leaders of the Puritans or the commanders of the Ironsides, in the Jacobin Club or at the head of the crowds that stormed the Bastille or invaded the Tuilleries. Nor did they seize the reins of government during the revolution, or for a long time afterwards, either in England or in France. . . . Yet the bourgeois character of these revolutions will not appear at all mythical if we approach them with a broader criterion and view their general impact on society. Their most substantial and enduring achievement was to sweep away the social and political institutions that had hindered the growth of bourgeois property and of the social relationships that went with it. . . . Bourgeois revolution creates the conditions in which bourgeois property can flourish. In this, rather than in the particular alignments during the struggle, lies its *differentia specifica*." *The Unfinished*

Revolution: Russia 1917–1967. Quoted in Christopher Hill, *Change and Continuity in Seventeenth Century England*, p. 280.

117. See Marx, "Guizot, 'Pourquoi la révolution d'Angleterre a-t-elle réussi?' " *CW* 10:254–55.

118. Hill argues that the economic divisions within the ranks of the direct producers were quickly on the way to becoming *class* divisions in the two generations before the Civil War. "Parliament and People in Seventeenth Century England," p. 119.

119. This argument draws largely upon Hill, "Parliament and People in Seventeenth Century England," pp. 107ff., and "A Bourgeois Revolution?" pp. 113ff.

120. Hill, "A Bourgeois Revolution?" p. 115. Stone offers an excellent discussion of the formation of the opposition to the Crown and the leadership role provided by the gentry in this struggle. See *The Causes of the English Revolution*, pp. 91–110.

121. Hill, *The Century of Revolution*, pp. 126–27.

122. Hill, *Reformation to Industrial Revolution*, p. 147.

123. Marx, *Capital* 1:676–78.

124. Stone, *The Causes of the English Revolution*, p. 72.

125. Kriedte, pp. 106–07.

126. Hill, *The Century of Revolution*, p. 162.

127. Moore, p. 77. An excellent summary of the peasants' final struggle against the ancien regime is provided by Goubert, *The Ancien Regime*, pp. 10–15.

128. See Skocpol, pp. 126–28.

129. Georges Lefebvre, "The Place of the Revolution in the Agrarian History of France," p. 34.

130. R. R. Palmer, "Georges Lefebvre: The Peasants and the French Revolution," p. 337.

131. Lefebvre, "The Place of the Revolution in the Agrarian History of France," pp. 41–43.

132. The principal sources for the following argument are Lucas, "Nobles, Bourgeois and the Origins of the French Revolution," pp. 122–30; and Skocpol, pp. 181–85. See also Lefebvre, *The Coming of the French Revolution*, pp. 159–61, Moore, pp. 77–80.

133. Lefebvre, *The Coming of the French Revolution*, pp. 155–68.

134. Kemp, *Economic Forces in French History*, p. 112; Soboul, "Classes and Class Struggles During the French Revolution," pp. 252–57; Moore, pp. 107–110. See also Marx's comments in *The Class Struggles in France*, *CW* 10:120–22; and *The Eighteenth Brumaire of Louis Bonaparte*, *CW* 11:187–92.

6

Conclusion

This study has sought to assess Marx's theory of history in light of the history of the transition from feudalism to capitalism. Its central aim was to initiate a reconstruction of Marx's theory: that is, to take apart its constituent concepts and recombine them in a way that is both faithful to their intent and historically accurate. We have seen that Marx oscillated between two incompatible versions of historical materialism: one emphasizes the explanatory primacy of class and class struggle, the other emphasizes the explanatory primacy of productive development. The historical study of feudalism and its supersession by capitalism provided a method to test their respective theoretical claims, to indicate, if possible, which Marx is right.

The first significant conclusion of this study is that the technological interpretation of historical materialism is belied by precapitalist modes of production. The main features of feudal class relations cannot be explained in terms of their role in promoting optimal productive development at the time. On the contrary, feudal class relations systematically blocked material progress. Furthermore, they produced an economic crisis which resulted in a prolonged regression of society's forces of production.

The thesis that history is the history of class struggle, in contrast, provided a cogent explanation of the feudal crisis complex. In this view, a crisis becomes manifest when the imperatives inherent in the existing class system and the requirements of maintaining a society's material base collide and cannot be reconciled. Feudal class struggle, we have seen, propelled the feudal economy, but only by means that eventually undermined the very prerequisites of continued growth. The lords were obliged to preserve the conditions of their rule by extracting from the peasant economy more surplus than they returned to it, eventually narrowing the base from which surplus could be drawn. Feudal rule compelled the peasantry to reproduce the economy under conditions which eroded its very viability. The eventual outcome, unintended and unwanted, was a dramatic contraction of the productive forces within the relations of production, evidenced in the fourteenth century feudal crisis and in the general crisis of the seventeenth century. Moreover, we have seen that productive expansion did not resume until feudal social relations were either restored or revamped: the centralized monarchy in France presided over an epoch of renewed feudal vigor, whereas early modern England witnessed economic growth under the aegis of nascent capitalist class relations.

The emergence of capitalism, however, appears at first sight to be more congenial to the technological interpretation of history. Capitalist class relations are a prodigious stimulus to material progress: competition requires capitalists to adopt a policy of innovation and productive investment. It seems reasonable to suggest, therefore, that capitalism arises and persists because it is uniquely able to promote the growth of humanity's productive power. Indeed, all of the historical illustrations Marx adduces to buttress the causal primacy of the productive forces are taken from the history of the rise of capitalist production. Moreover, a tradition of economic history dating back to classical political economy explains the emergence of capitalism in terms of its impact on and suitability for economic growth. Marx's early historical works belong to this tradition. Nevertheless, we have argued that Marx abandoned this form of explanation in his mature economic histories in favor of an analysis which privileges long-term processes of class struggle and class formation.

Now, G. A. Cohen maintains that Marx's later writings offer

an account of the genesis of capitalist class relations which accords with the technological interpretation of history. The focus of Cohen's reading is Part VIII of Volume 1 of *Capital*, specifically, Marx's summary of his study of the process of primitive capital accumulation that underwrote the rise of the capitalist mode of production.[1] According to Marx, as we have seen, the locus and classical case of this process was the English countryside. Its essential feature was the expropriation, effected chiefly by enclosure, of independent peasant cultivators from the soil. This process culminated in the formation of a working class, individuals owning nothing but their labor power, facing a capitalist class, exclusive owners of the means of production.

Cohen points out that Marx's narrative begins with the economy of small peasant holdings. That is, it begins *after* the demise of serfdom proper. Marx says very little here about the transition from serfdom to petty proprietorship; his primary preoccupation is with the next transition, from widespread small holding to capitalism. The economy of independent peasant cultivators, Marx argues, gave rise to a potential for economic growth it was incompetent to realize. The type of property rights defining peasant agriculture precluded the concentration of the means of production and the rationalization of the work process, excluding new forces from the productive sphere. Hence: "It must be annihilated; it is annihilated."[2] Into its place stepped capitalist class relations, more apt to promote and therefore necessary for optimal productive development.

Cohen's interpretation reveals precisely the nature of the logic required to establish the sovereignty of the productive forces. Its main weakness is its starting point. Cohen begins his discussion of Marx's analysis of the emergence of capitalism with the productive forces created by the economy of petty proprietorship. That is, he *assumes* a given level of material progress, quite independent of the class struggles which generated it. Marx's study of the historical processes which yielded the petty mode of production are ignored. Cohen then deduces from the existing productive forces a class with the capacity and the interest to maximize productivity, suggesting that capitalist class relations prevailed because they realized that interest.

The technological interpretation of history thus makes an arbitrary entrance into the historical process: the forces of production are taken in isolation, abstracted from their historical antecedents, and made to precede the social relations. This method provides a license to conceive any social formation as a response to a certain level of progress of the forces of production, but only because this level is arbitrarily made the starting point of historical investigation. Indeed, this is the same method Marx employs, when generalizing about history, to produce the thesis that a society's productive forces explain its relations of production. Its logic is encapsulated in Marx's formula:

> If you assume a given state of development of man's productive faculties, you will have a corresponding form of commerce and consumption. If you assume given stages of development in production, commerce or consumption, you will have a corresponding form of social constitution, a corresponding organization, whether of the family, of the estates or of the classes—in a word, a corresponding civil society.[3]

Capitalist class relations are, of course, conducive to economic growth. But Cohen's defense of Marx's theory of history requires him to show that capitalist class relations arose *because* they were the most conducive at the time.[4] He can do so only by revising Marx's theory of class in a way that Marx does not normally countenance. On this reading, a class is composed of individuals possessing a capacity and an interest that is more fundamental than their capacity and interest to maximize surplus appropriation—namely, the ability and desire to overcome material scarcity. Being rational, individuals are bound, predictably, to maximize productivity, given the technologies available to them. Class behavior reflects this imperative: classes respond in the first instance to the exigencies of production. This conception of class is essential to the technological interpretation because it ensures that, at the decisive moment, a class will appear which is best able and disposed to promote maximum economic progress. This class will correspond to and therefore be "selected" by the functional requirements of the development of the productive forces. Classes succeed and rule because they are best suited to develop the economy at the time. Revolutionary classes overturn existing class relations when the latter inhibit economic progress. They assume a position of power because their mode of exploitation is more productive than that of any other competitor; less productive classes are inevitably defeated by more productive ones. Accordingly, a particular mode of exploitation is obtained and prevails because it is the most conducive to economic development. In this view, surplus extraction is not, or not primarily, a function of class power, but rather of a class's contribution to maximizing technological development.

Marx's actual historical researches, however, assign explanatory primacy to class struggle, sharply contradicting the technological interpretation of his theory of history. These studies always take into account the processes of class conflict and class formation underlying material progress. That is, they do not assume the existence of a specific scheme of the productive forces as given, conceiving its historical antecedents as tabula rasa, but rather seek to explain this scheme by investigating the historical conditions which gave rise to it and within which it developed. The conception of class used here is that entailed in the thesis that history is the history of class struggle.

Marx's mature historical analyses trace the rise of capitalism to the decline of feudalism. He examines the resolution of feudal class struggle in Volume 3 of *Capital*.[5] Viewed from the perspective of Volume 3, an interpretation of Part VIII of Volume 1 emerges which belies Cohen's reading of it. Thus whereas, as Cohen points out, Marx's narrative of the formation of capitalist class relations begins with the economy of petty agricultural producers, Marx does not, as Cohen claims he does, *explain* the internal dynamic of this economy in terms of the development of productive capacities it is incompetent to realize. Quite the contrary, Marx explains the genesis and subsequent fate of the petty mode of production by first locating it within the process of decline of feudalism. In other words, he examines the transition from petty proprietorship to capitalist private property only in the context of the transition from serfdom to widespread small holdings. This is precisely the context that Cohen neglects to study. Marx, however, contends that it is the prior dissolution of feudal class relations that "set free the elements" that recombined to form capitalist class relations.[6]

We have seen that independent small holdings were the

product of successful peasant class struggle against the feudal aristocracy, which irreparably impaired lordly power, emancipating the peasantry. The triumph of the peasants as a class, however, produced two closely related results. First, it led to the economic florescence of peasant agriculture. The newly independent cultivators were enabled to retain a major portion of their surplus and to employ it freely, unencumbered by disruptive feudal exactions. The petty mode of production was thus permitted room to flourish, to let loose its whole energy. Secondly, however, the emancipation of the peasantry led to its disintegration as a class. These twin eventualities set the stage for the primitive accumulation of capital. Many of the formerly defeated lords and gentlemen were enabled to recoup their lost fortunes in an entirely new fashion: they forcibly evicted the peasantry from the soil. They were obliged to do so because the possibility of reimposing feudal controls over the cultivators was closed to them. The peasants had effectively put an end to this mode of extracting an economic surplus. The gentry was successful not because it controlled superior productive forces, but rather because the peasants were no longer capable of resisting expropriation as a cohesive class. Improving lords thus employed the new agricultural techniques pioneered by the petty producers on their enclosed lands. The genesis of capitalist class relations established the imperatives which yielded systematic increases in productivity. In short, only these *prior* changes in class relations, Marx suggests, generated a new set of productive forces, and not vice versa.

It is now possible to identify the source of these two versions of historical materialism in Marx's texts. Marx's theory of class, we have seen, rigorously distinguishes a person's position with respect to the productive forces from his position with respect to the relations of production. The two constituent elements of a mode of production have very different implications for a class's composition and interests. The place individuals come to occupy in the scheme of the productive forces forms the practical basis of their talent and capacity for organization as a class. Thus, for example, the patterns of land use and technology among peasants in medieval Europe gave rise to their capacity for concerted action. The continuous cooperation among villagers required to administer the agricultural system wove the cultivators into a cohesive class. In a similar vein, Marx showed that the grouping of workers by capitalism's factory system, and their organization in assembly lines, work shifts, labor teams, and so on, is one of the principal sources of working class formation, equipping the proletariat with its capacity for class struggle.[7]

It is the place individuals come to occupy in society's ownership relations, however, which determines their predicament and their interests as a class. Their disposition to think and behave in class ways is rooted in and animated by the conflict of interest over the distribution of socially produced wealth. Thus, medieval peasants developed a sense of the distinctive interests they shared in the course of repeated clashes with the lords over the appropriation of their labor and its product. Similarly, Marx argues that wage laborers find and articulate the common language of their class in the process of sharpening their struggle against the imperatives of capitalist exploitation.[8] The aim of individuals within these subordinate classes, in terms of which they are defined and in turn define themselves as a class, is their common interest in wresting from their superiors greater control over their labor power and its product.

Ruling classes, for their part, have an overriding interest in preserving society's property system and not, or not primarily, in developing its forces of production. To be sure, ruling classes and systems of exploitation do make contributions to productive development. However, it is the position individuals occupy as members of a ruling class which obliges them to make whatever economic contributions they make. Their economic role derives from the strategies they are compelled to adopt to maintain the conditions of their rule, that is, from their capacities and needs as exploiters, not from the imperatives of technological progress. The maximization of surplus appropriation is not equivalent for the maximization of productive development. This is the conclusion yielded by Marx's study of merchant capitalism. The encouragement merchants gave to economic growth was both determined and circumscribed by their place in the network of feudal ownership relations. Accordingly, despite their role in developing society's productive forces,

Marx maintains that merchants were ultimately conservative, wedded to the preservation of the feudal regime as the precondition of their ability to extract an economic surplus.

In a similar vein, the nascent agrarian capitalists of early modern England triumphed not because they were the class best suited to develop the productive forces, nor because they commanded the most advanced forces at the time. As we have seen, the success of peasant class struggle obliged the lords to develop new means of appropriating a surplus; those who failed were ruined. Clearly, the nascent property arrangements *were* admirably suited to the systematic development of the productive forces. But this is not to say that they obtained and prevailed *because* they were thus suited. The dissolution of the petty mode of production created a market in tenants. Not only were tenants thereby compelled to maximize production or be replaced by more able brethren, but landlords were required to compete to attract the better tenants. This competition forced landlords to encourage productive development—for example, to cooperate with tenants in bearing the cost of agricultural improvements. The new capitalist landlords assumed a lead in agricultural improvements because they were capitalists; they did not become capitalists because they were leaders in agriculture.[9]

The technological interpretation of historical materialism, however, confuses the different ways in which individuals are "carriers" of their class on the one hand, and of the productive forces on the other. In this view, the position individuals occupy in society's forces of production is not only the concrete ground of their potential for concerted action as a class, it determines the aim and end of their struggle as well. Marx thus establishes the primacy of the productive forces by slipping from an examination of the ways in which the utilization of any given technology facilitates the consolidation of class relationships, to the suggestion that it determines the motive force of class interests as well. Underlying this slippage is "the premise that the satisfaction of human physical-biological needs is the most continuous and compelling of all man's activities, hence the prerequisite to all others."[10] Classes, then, embody a historical project "given" to them by the stage of development achieved by the productive forces. "For the oppressed class to be able to emancipate itself," Marx writes, "it is necessary that the productive powers already acquired and the existing social relations should no longer be capable of existing side by side. Of all the instruments of production, the greatest productive power is the revolutionary class itself."[11]

Why, then, was Marx not aware that he offered two incompatible versions of historical materialism? One reason, it may be argued, is that in the main historical example of qualitative social transformation Marx looked to—the transition from feudalism to capitalism—the new class system coincided to an unprecedented degree with material progress. "The bourgeoisie," he wrote, "cannot exist without constantly revolutionising the instruments of production."[12] This statement clearly lends itself to the view that vigorous bourgeois forces of production burst triumphantly through retrograde feudal relations of production to establish a higher productivity on their ruins. Hence Cohen argues that capitalism best exemplifies the technological interpretation, when this interpretation is functionally construed.[13] The bourgeoisie appears to embody new productive forces: Steam power is equivalent to society with the industrial capitalist. This conclusion is possible, however, because the nascent capitalist class is the only class in world history to institutionalize self-sustaining economic growth. For the capitalist class, and only for this class, emancipation from the social and economic dominance of the feudal regime coincided with productive development. The technological interpretation of historical materialism, then, appears to be a misreading of a particular conjuncture between class relations and the forces of production, which was then generalized into a historical law. Marx's theory of class struggle avoids both this misreading and this generalization.

Marx's theory of class, however, must itself be amended in order to faithfully reconstruct the logic of the transition from feudalism to capitalism. Specifically, the analysis of radical social change has revealed a distinction between two types of class struggle: The antagonism within a class system and that between class systems. These two forms of conflict have different sources and there is no inherent connection between them. They comprise distinct ways in which the contending classes are defined and in turn define themselves in relation to each other. Specifically, the way in which class oppression is experienced in these two types of class relationship is very different, opening entirely divergent possibilities for social change.

We have seen that the antagonism within a mode of production, arising out of the system of exploitation, accurately explains a society's internal dynamic. This antagonism does not explain, however, the genesis and formation of a revolutionary class. Marx rightly claimed that individuals are led and accustomed to organize and to struggle as a class by the experience of common conditions of exploitation. But, equally importantly, their collective identity as a class is *circumscribed* by the conditions they organize to combat. Their success as a class, that is, in destroying these conditions, therefore spells the end of the need to act in concert and the class dissolves. Thus, if the peasants in Western Europe constituted themselves as a successful class against the lords, their triumph made manifest the limits of their cohesion as a class. The rationale for concerted peasant action disappeared with the defeat of the aristocracy.

This conclusion questions the Marxian assumption that the emancipation of an oppressed class (in this sense) entails the formation of a wholly new society.[14] It is more correct to view its emancipation as resulting in the dissolution of the existing society, that is, in "the common ruin of the contending classes."[15] Far from vitiating Marx's class analysis as a whole, however, this historical outcome argues for a more tenable reconceptualization of class and class struggle. For Marx argues that class is a *relationship* in which individuals experience and articulate the identity of their collective interests only in the process of being compelled to struggle against other individuals whose interests are antagonistic to theirs. This notion implies that when the class relationship is broken as a result of the triumph of the oppressed class, the basis of class cohesion withers and the class necessarily falls apart.

The class antagonism within a mode of production contrasts sharply with that characteristic of the clash between modes of production. If peasant class struggle was circumscribed by the need to destroy the feudal regime, the nascent bourgeoisie succeeded in replacing it with the regime of private property, successfully constituting itself as an alternative ruling class. To be sure, we have seen that the nascent bourgeoisie was internally divided; various fractions articulated different objectives. Many bourgeois sought to find a place within the old order, to make compromises with it, even to restore it and make it work, particularly when they contemplated the popular rebellions unleashed by their activities. Yet the movement for compromise and reform necessarily stopped short. On the one hand, the existing regime provided little room for flexibility: Threatened from below, increasingly ossified and unable to govern, it concentrated on the defense of the traditional prerogatives upon which its rule depended. On the other hand, the class identity of the individuals who came to form the new class was determined by their relationship to a wholly new type of property in the means of production. If the bourgeoisie formed a subordinate class within the feudal regime, it was in the sense that feudal property arrangements militated against the consolidation of the new property form. The aim and end of the contending classes, by which they are defined and in terms of which they came to define themselves as classes, had its source in the need of the emerging bourgeoisie to dissolve the social and economic relationships of feudal rule, and the aristocracy to restore and preserve them. Consequently, increasing numbers of individuals among the bourgeoisie came to measure their oppression, however vaguely, not in terms of the surplus extracted from them, but rather in terms of the real possibility of constructing an alternative society, by reference to which they progressively distanced themselves from their given circumstances, and found them to be capricious and unjust. Nascent ownership relations established the possibility and the limit of productive development in new social formations.

NOTES

1. See G. A. Cohen, *Karl Marx's Theory of History*, pp. 176–80. Marx's summary appears on pp. 713–15.
2. Marx, Vol. 1 of *Capital*, p. 714.

3. Marx, Letter to Annenkov, 28 December 1846, in Vol. 38 of Marx and Engles, *Collected Works*, p. 96. (Hereafter *CW*.) An incisive critique of this formula is provided by Sahlins, *Culture and Practical Reason*, pp. 146–47.

4. G. A. Cohen, *Karl Marx's Theory of History*, pp. 180–81, 280–93.

5. Marx, Vol. 3 of *Capital*, pp. 796–802. This analysis is examined above, in Chapter 4.

6. Marx, *Capital* 1:668.

7. Marx, *Manifesto of the Communist Party*, *CW* 6:490–94.

8. Marx, *Capital* 1:224–25.

9. See Marx, *Capital* 1:314–15.

10. Sahlins, *Culture and Practical Reason*, p. 146. This premise plays a central role in Cohen's defense of the primacy of the productive forces: see *Karl Marx's Theory of History*, pp. 150–53.

11. Marx, *The Poverty of Philosophy* *CW* 6:211.

12. Marx, *Manifesto of the Communist Party*, *CW* 6:487.

13. G. A. Cohen, *Karl Marx's Theory of History*, p. 170.

14. "An oppressed class," writes Marx, "is the vital condition for every society founded on the antagonism of classes. The emancipation of the oppressed class thus implies necessarily the creation of a new society." *The Poverty of Philosophy*, *CW* 6:211.

15. Marx, *Manifesto of the Communist Party*, *CW* 6:482.

Selected Bibliography

PRIMARY SOURCES

Marx, Karl. *Capital.* Translated by Samuel Moore and Edward Aveling and edited by Frederick Engels. 3 vols. Moscow: Progress Publishers, n.d.

———. *Grundrisse.* Translated by Martin Nicolaus. Harmondsworth: Penguin Books, 1973.

Marx, Karl, and Frederick Engels. *Collected Works.* 50 vols. projected. Moscow: Progress Publishers, 1975-.

———. *Selected Correspondence.* 3d rev. ed. Moscow: Progress Publishers, 1975.

Tucker, Robert C., ed. *The Marx-Engels Reader.* 2d ed. New York: W. W. Norton, 1978.

SECONDARY SOURCES

Anderson, Perry. *Arguments Within English Marxism.* London: New Left Books, 1980.

———. *In the Tracks of Historical Materialism.* Chicago: The University of Chicago Press, 1984.

———. *Lineages of the Absolutist State.* London: New Left Books, 1974.

———. *Passages from Antiquity to Feudalism.* London: New Left Books, 1974.

Andrew, Edward. "Class in Itself and Class Against Capital: Karl Marx and his Classifiers." *Canadian Journal of Political Science* 16 (September 1983): 577–584.

Aston, T. H., editor. *Crisis in Europe, 1560–1660*. New York: Basic Books, 1965.

Aston, T. H., and C. H. E. Philpin, editors. *The Brenner Debate, Agrarian Class Structure and Economic Development in Pre-Industrial Europe*. Cambridge: Cambridge University Press, 1987.

Ball, Terrence, and James Farr, editors. *After Marx*. Cambridge: Cambridge University Press, 1984.

Bloch, Marc. *French Rural History, An Essay on its Basic Characteristics*. Translated by Janet Sondheimer. Los Angeles: University of California Press, 1966.

———. "The Rise of Dependent Cultivation and Seigniorial Institutions." In *The Agrarian Life of the Middle Ages*. Vol. 1 of *The Cambridge Economic History of Europe*. Edited by J. H. Clapham and Eileen Power. Cambridge: Cambridge University Press, 1944.

Bois, Guy. *The Crisis of Feudalism, Economy and Society in Eastern Normandy c. 1300–1550*. Cambridge: Cambridge University Press, and Paris: Editions de la Maison des Sciences de l'Homme, 1984.

Braudel, Fernand. *The Structures of Everyday Life*. Translated by Sian Reynolds. New York: Harper and Row, 1981.

———. *The Wheels of Commerce*. Translated by Sian Reynolds. New York: Harper and Row, 1982.

Brenner, Robert. "The Origins of Capitalist Development: a Critique of Neo-Smithian Marxism." *New Left Review* 104 (July–August 1977): 25–92.

Brenner, Robert. "The Social Basis of Economic Development." In *Analytical Marxism*. Edited by John Roemer. Cambridge: Cambridge University Press, and Paris: Editions de la Maison des Sciences de l'Homme, 1986.

Bridbury, A. R. *Economic Growth, England in the Later Middle Ages*. Sussex: The Harvester Press, 1975.

Chavance, Bernard, editor. *Marx en Perspective*. Paris: Éditions de l'École des Hautes Études en Science Sociales, 1983.

Cipolla, Carlo M. *Before the Industrial Revolution, European Society and Economy, 1000–1700*. 2d ed. New York: W. W. Norton, 1980.

Clark, Peter, editor. *Country Towns in Pre-Industrial England*. Leicester: Leicester University Press, 1981.

Clark, Peter, and Paul Slack, editors. *Crisis and Order in English Towns, 1500–1700*. Toronto: University of Toronto Press, 1972.

———. *English Towns in Transition, 1500–1700*. Oxford: University Press, 1976.

Clarkson, L. A. *The Pre-Industrial Economy in England, 1500–1750.* New York: Schocken Books, 1971.

Cobban, Alfred. *A History of Modern France.* 3 vols. Harmondsworth: Penguin Books, 1963.

———. *The Social Interpretation of the French Revolution.* Cambridge: Cambridge University Press, 1964.

Cohen, G. A. "Functional Explanation, Consequence Explanation, and Marxism." *Inquiry* 25 (March 1982): 27–56.

———. "Forces and Relations of Production," in *Analytical Marxism.* Edited by John Roemer. Cambridge: Cambridge University Press, 1968.

———. *Karl Marx's Theory of History: A Defence* Princeton: Princeton University Press, 1978.

———. "Reply to Four Critics." *Analyse & Kritik* 5(1983): 195–222.

Cohen, Joshua, "Review of *Karl Marx's Theory of History: A Defence.*" *The Journal of Philosophy* 79(May 1982):253–273.

Colletti, Lucio. *From Rousseau to Lenin.* Translated by John Merrington and Judith White. New York: Monthly Review Press, 1972.

Darnton, Robert. *The Great Cat Massacre and Other Episodes in French Cultural History.* New York: Basic Books, 1984.

Draper, Hal. *Karl Marx's Theory of Revolution.* 2 vols. New York: Monthly Review Press, 1977–1978.

Dobb, Maurice. *Studies in the Development of Capitalism.* New York: International Publishers, 1963.

Elster, Jon. *Making Sense of Marx.* Cambridge: Cambridge University Press, and Paris: Editions de la Maison des Sciences de l'Homme, 1985.

Fletcher, A. J. "Parliament and People in Seventeenth Century England." *Past and Present* 98(February 1983): 151–155.

Fox-Genovese, Elizabeth, and Eugene D. Genovese. *Fruits of Merchant Capital.* Oxford: Oxford Univ. Press, 1983.

Giddens, Anthony. *Capitalism and Modern Social Theory.* Cambridge: Cambridge University Press, 1971.

———. *The Class Structure of the Advanced Societies.* London: Hutchinson University Library, 1973.

Goubert, Pierre. "Local History." In *Historical Studies Today.* Edited by Felix Gilbert and S. R. Graubard. New York: W. W. Norton, 1972.

———. *The Ancien Regime, French Society 1600–1750.* Translated by Steve Cox. New York: Harper and Row, 1973.

Habermas, Jurgen. *Communication and the Evolution of Society.* Translated by Thomas McCarthy. Boston: Beacon Press, 1979.

———. *Knowledge and Human Interests*. Translated by Jeremy Shapiro. Boston: Beacon Press, 1978.

Hexter, J. H. *Reappraisals in History*. London: Longmans, Green and Co., 1961.

Hibbert, A. B. "The Economic Policies of Towns." In *Economic Organization and Policies in the Middle Ages*. Vol. 3 of *The Cambridge Economic History of Europe*. Edited by M. M. Postan, E. E. Rich, and Edward Miller. Cambridge: Cambridge University Press, 1963.

———. "The Origins of the Medieval Town Patriciate." *Past and Present* 3 (February):15–27.

Hill, Christopher. *The Century of Revolution, 1603–1714*. New York: W. W. Norton, 1980.

———. *Change and Continuity in Seventeenth Century England*. Cambridge: Cambridge University Press, 1975.

———. "Parliament and People in Seventeenth Century England." *Past and Present* 92 (August 1981): 100–124.

———. *Puritanism and Revolution*. London: Secker and Warburg, 1958.

———. *Reformation to Industrial Revolution*. Harmondsworth: Penguin Books, 1969.

Hilton, Rodney, H. *Bond Men Made Free, Medieval Peasant Movements and the English Rising of 1381*. London: Methuen, 1973.

———. *The Decline of Serfdom in Medieval England*. New York: St. Martin's Press, 1969.

———. *The English Peasantry in the Later Middle Ages*. Oxford: Oxford University Press, 1975.

———. "Feudalism in Europe: Problems for Historical Materialists." *New Left Review* 147 (September–October 1984): 84–93.

———. "Medieval Market Towns and Simple Commodity Production." *Past and Present* 109 (November 1985): 3–23.

———. *A Medieval Society*. London: Weidenfeld and Nicolson, 1966.

———, editor. *The Transition From Feudalism to Capitalism*. London: New Left Books, 1976.

———. "Warriors and Peasants." *New Left Review* 83 (January–February 1973): 83–94.

Hobsbawm, Eric. *Industry and Empire*. Harmondsworth: Penguin Books, 1969.

Johnson, Douglas, editor. *French Society and the Revolution*. Cambridge: Cambridge University Press, 1976.

Jones, E. L., editor. *Agriculture and Economic Growth in England, 1650–1815*. London: Methuen, 1967.

———. *Agriculture and the Industrial Revolution.* New York: John Wiley and Sons, 1974.

Kemp, Tom. *Economic Forces in French History.* London: Dobson Books, 1971.

Kolakowski, Leszek. *Main Currents of Marxism.* 3 vols. Translated by P. S. Falla. Oxford: Oxford University Press, 1978.

Kriedte, Peter. *Peasants, Landlords and Merchant Capitalists. Europe and the World Economy, 1500–1800.* Translated by V. R. Berghahn. Cambridge: Cambridge University Press, 1983.

Lefebvre, Georges. *The Coming of the French Revolution.* Translated by R. R. Palmer. Princeton: Princeton University Press, 1947.

———. *The Great Fear.* Translated by Joan White. London: New Left Books, 1973.

———. "The Place of the Revolution in the Agrarian History of France." In *Rural Society in France.* Edited by Robert Forster and Orest Ranum. Translated by Elborg Forster and Patricia M. Ranum. Baltimore: The Johns Hopkins University Press, 1977.

Le Roy Ladurie, Emmanuel. *The Peasants of Languedoc.* Translated and introduced by John Day. Chicago: University of Illinois Press, 1974.

Levine, Andrew, and Erik Olin Wright. "Rationality and Class Struggle." *New Left Review* 123 (September–October 1980): 47–68.

Levine, David. *Family Formation in an Age of Nascent Capitalism.* New York: Academic Press, 1977.

Lublinskaya, A. D. *French Absolutism: The Crucial Phase, 1620–1629.* Translated by Brian Pearce. Cambridge: Cambridge University Press, 1968.

Macpherson, C. B. *The Political Theory of Possessive Individualism: Hobbes to Locke.* Oxford: Oxford University Press, 1962.

McMurtry, John. *The Structure of Marx's World-View.* Princeton: Princeton University Press, 1978.

Miller, Richard, W. *Analyzing Marx.* Princeton: Princeton University Press, 1984.

Moore, Barrington, Jr. *Social Origins of Dictatorship and Democracy.* Boston: Beacon Press, 1966.

Palmer, R. R. "Georges Lefebvre: The Peasants and the French Revolution." *Journal of Modern History* 31 (December 1959): 329–342.

Parker, Geoffrey, and Lesley M. Smith, editors. *The General Crisis of the Seventeenth Century.* London: Routledge and Kegan Paul, 1978.

Pirenne, Henri. *Economic and Social History of Medieval Europe.* New York: Harcourt, Brace and World, 1937.

———. *A History of Europe, from the Invasions to the XVI Century*. London: Allen and Unwin, 1939.
———. *Medieval Cities, Their Origins and the Revival of Trade*. Princeton: Princeton University Press, 1925.
———. *The Stages in the Social History of Capitalism*. Social Science Papers, No. 1. Stanford: Academic Reprints, 1953.
Pocock, J. G. A., editor. *Three British Revolutions: 1641, 1688, 1776*. Princeton: Princeton University Press, 1980.
Postan, M. M. *The Medieval Economy and Society*. London: Weidenfeld and Nicolson, 1972.
Printz, Arthur M. "Background and Ulterior Motive of Marx's Preface of 1859." *Journal of the History of Ideas* 30 (1969): 437–450.
Rabb, Theodore K. *The Struggle for Stability in Early Modern Europe*. New York: Oxford University Press, 1975.
Rigby, S. H. *Marxism and History. A Critical Introduction*. St. Martin's Press, 1987.
Roemer, John, editor. *Analytical Marxism*. Cambridge: Cambridge University Press, and Paris: Editions de la Maison des Sciences de l'Homme, 1986.
Sahlins, Marshall. *Culture and Practical Reason*. Chicago: University of Chicago Press, 1976.
Sartre, Jean-Paul. *Search for a Method*. Translated by Hazel E. Barnes. New York: Vintage Books, 1968.
Shaw, William H. *Marx's Theory of History*. Stanford: Stanford University Press, 1978.
Skocpol, Theda. *States and Social Revolutions*. Cambridge: Cambridge University Press, 1979.
———, editor. *Vision and Method in Historical Sociology*. Cambridge: Cambridge University Press, 1984.
Smith, Adam. *The Wealth of Nations*. Edited by Andrew Skinner. Harmondsworth: Penguin Books, 1970, 1974.
Soboul, Albert. "Classes and Class Struggles During the French Revolution." *Science and Society* 17(1953): 257–283.
———. *The Parisian Sans-Culottes and the French Revolutions, 1793–4*. Translated by Guynne Lewis. London: Oxford University Press, 1964.
———. "Persistence of 'Feudalism' in the Rural Society of Nineteenth-Century France." In *Rural Society in France*. Edited by Robert Forster and Orest Ranum. Translated by Elborg Forster and Patricia M. Ranum. Baltimore: The Johns Hopkins University Press, 1977.
Steuart, Sir James. *An Inquiry into the Principles of Political Economy*. Ed-

ited and introduced by Andrew S. Skinner. 2 vols. London: Oliver and Boyd, 1966.

Stone, Lawrence. "The Bourgeois Revolution of Seventeenth Century England Revisited." *Past and Present* 109(November 1985): 44–54.

———. *The Causes of the English Revolution, 1529–1642*. New York: Harper and Row, 1972.

Supple, Barry. "The Nature of Enterprise." In *The Economic Organization of Early Modern Europe*. Vol. 5 of *The Cambridge Economic History of Europe*. Edited by E. E. Rich and C. H. Wilson. Cambridge: Cambridge University Press, 1977.

Tawney, R. H. "The Rise of the Gentry, 1558–1640." In *Essays in Economic History*. Edited by E. E. Carus-Wilson. Vol. 1. London: Edward Arnold, 1954.

Taylor, George V. "Non-Capitalist Wealth and the Origins of the French Revolution." *American Historical Review* 72(January 1967): 469–496.

———. "Types of Capitalism in Eighteenth-Century France." *English Historical Review* 79(July 1964): 478–497.

Thirsk, Joan. "The Common Fields." In *Peasants, Knights and Heretics*. Edited by Rodney Hilton. Cambridge: Cambridge University Press, 1976.

Thompson, E. P. "Eighteenth Century English Society: Class Struggle Without Class?" *Social History* 3(May 1978): 133–165.

———. *The Making of the English Working Class*. Harmondsworth: Penguin Books, 1968.

———. *The Poverty of Theory and Other Essays*. London: Merlin Press, 1978.

Trevor-Roper, H. R. "The Gentry, 1540–1640." In *Economic History Review*. Supplement No. 1 (1953): 1–15. Published for the Economic History Society by Cambridge University Press, Cambridge.

Tuchmann, Barbara W. *A Distant Mirror, The Calamitous 14th Century*. New York: Ballantine Books, 1978.

Unwin, George. *Industrial Organization in the Sixteenth and Seventeenth Centuries*. Introduction by T. S. Aston. Reprints of Economic Classics. New York: Augustus M. Kelley, 1971.

Wallerstein, Immanuel. "From Feudalism to Capitalism: Transition or Transitions?" *Social Forces* 55(December 1976): 273–283.

———. *The Modern World System*. 2 vols. New York: Academic Press, 1974, 1980.

———."The Rise and Future Demise of the World Capitalist System:

Concepts for Comparative Analysis." *Comparative Studies In Society and History* 16(September 1974): 387–415.

Weber, Max. *The City*. Translated and edited by Don Martindale and Gertrud Neuwith. Glencoe: The Free Press, 1958.

———. *General Economic History*. Translated by Frank H. Knight. Glencoe: The Free Press, 1927.

White, Lynn, Jr. *Medieval Technology and Social Change*. Oxford: Oxford University Press, 1962.

Wilson, C. H. "The Historical Study of Growth and Decline in Early Modern Europe." In *The Economic Organization of Early Modern Europe*. Vol. 5 of *The Cambridge Economic History of Europe*. Ed. E. E. Rich and C. H. Wilson. Cambridge: Cambridge University Press, 1977.

Wood, Ellen Meiksins. "Marxism and the Course of History." *New Left Review* 147(September-October, 1984): 95–107.

———. "The Politics of Theory and the Concept of Class: E. P. Thompson and His Critics." *Studies in Political Economy* 9(Fall 1982): 45–75.

Wood, Ellen Meiksins, and Neal Wood. *Class Ideology and Ancient Political Theory*. New York: Oxford University Press, 1978.

Zagorin, Perez. "The Social Interpretation of the English Revolution." *Journal of Economic History* 19 (September 1959): 376–401.

Index

The names of Marx and Engels have been omitted from the index.

About the Author

CLAUDIO J. KATZ is an Assistant Professor of Political Science at Loyola University of Chicago

Printed by Libri Plureos GmbH in Hamburg,
Germany

9 780313 264238